Overflow

Kenny
Luck

Overflow

**Setting the Holy
Spirit Loose in the
World You Live In**

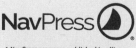

A NavPress resource published in alliance
with Tyndale House Publishers

NavPress ◑

NavPress is the publishing ministry of The Navigators, an international Christian organization and leader in personal spiritual development. NavPress is committed to helping people grow spiritually and enjoy lives of meaning and hope through personal and group resources that are biblically rooted, culturally relevant, and highly practical.

For more information, visit NavPress.com.

CONTENTS

Every man is a missionary, now and forever, for good or for evil, whether he intends or designs it or not. He may be a blot radiating his dark influence outward to the very circumference of society, or he may be a blessing spreading benediction over the length and breadth of the world; but a blank he cannot be. There are no moral blanks, there are no neutral characters; we are either the leaven that sours and corrupts, or the light that splendidly illuminates, and the salt that silently operates; but being dead, as being alive, every man speaks.

JOHN CUMMING

INTRODUCTION

The Overarching Tale

WE WANT TO KNOW where things are leading. Rare is the man who says to himself, "I don't need to know what's next," or "I'm good with whatever happens." Human beings like predictability too much for that to be a natural response to new environments, new relationships, or new processes beyond our control. Key word? *New.*

Or more accurately, *unknown.*

Like me, most men are not fans of engaging anything unfamiliar, mysterious, or beyond their personal knowledge. The jump from the known to the unknown produces a pause in us that very quickly leads to questions like:

- So what did you say goes on at this meeting?
- Who is going to be there?
- Where are they having it?
- Are they serving food?
- What is going to happen exactly?
- What is going to be the topic of discussion?
- How long will it last?
- How much does it cost?
- Why should I go?

Our *time* is the coin of the realm—we value it and spend it wisely because once it is gone, we can't un-spend it. It's not that we never want to try new things, but if we are going to be placed in an unfamiliar setting with unfamiliar faces and an unknown process with undefined goals, well, we are *out*.

We need answers.

Whenever I am talking to a man and he is asking about our men's community at Crossline Church, the church I serve, I provide answers to these and other questions *before he even asks them*. I want his brain to work from the *known* to the unknown. Consequently, in the most direct and dispassionate way possible, I tell him what he can expect to happen *before* it happens. I share:

- How connecting with other men is routine and easy
- What a gathering or group experience is like
- What the first meeting (especially) will entail
- How the ninety minutes of time is structured *exactly*
- How many weeks each module/topic will take
- How the leader development journey has a clear goal
- What personal knowledge or benefits he will leave with
- What my goals and hopes are for his process

No rah-rah speech needed. Slay the dragon—his fear of the unknown.

When I've said this in the thousands of recruiting conversations I have had, I've seen a look of relief on many faces. I learned a long time ago that a man will show up once to most anything if the perceived risk is low and there is a strong benefit. On the primal level, that could simply be good barbecued tri-tip at the Beast Feast we hold each spring at Crossline (five hundred pounds of choice, custom-smoked tri-tip). On the relational level, that could be a much-needed increase in intimacy with his wife or children at our Get Healthy modules. On an inner level, it could be defeating an ongoing character issue that is harming his relationships with God and people he loves. On the spiritual level, it could be his need for a structured and strong spiritual-growth journey that is long overdue. On a leadership level, it could be a desire to start or participate in a ministry in the church.

But once he shows up in a space built for that benefit to be realized and starts that journey, a dormant part of his brain is activated. A deeper, more subconscious question in his head starts percolating. After showing up, he looks around, assesses, engages, and maybe even participates. But like a beach ball being strenuously held under the water, an invisible but inevitable question pops up in his mind: *Now that you have me, where are you taking me?*

We want to know the outcome of the process.

We are also subconsciously hoping it is a *great one*.

God's Endgame

The human soul is attracted to superhumanity and the larger super-story. For proof, look no further than the Marvel Cinematic Universe (MCU). To help the uninitiated (should they exist), the MCU is the shared place where all the movie adaptations of Marvel comic book stories are set. The "A Team" members of this realm are known as the Avengers—Captain America, Captain Marvel, Iron Man, Thor, Black Panther, Black Widow, Hawkeye, the Hulk, Ant-Man, and the Wasp. The "B Team" is a seemingly endless cast of characters who serendipitously and purposefully fold into the super-story with their own skills, personalities, and humor. Each character has his or her own distinct story and ever important backstory that also intersects and connects with other past, present, or developing stories in the MCU—*all to tell a single, overarching tale.*

As of August 2021, this unified collection of fantasy adventures is the largest box-office supernova of all time. Judging by ticket sales and sheer number of films, it has more pull, accessibility, and resonance than J. K. Rowling's and George Lucas's mysterious and magical forces.[1] Marvel's ethos of superhumanness dwarfs its nearest competitors.

I know *the pull* on an intimate level. In fact, my earliest memories of it look like a four-year-old relentlessly hounding his exhausted mother of seven kids for outfits, toy accessories, pajamas, toothbrushes, lunch pails, board games, underwear, and even soap (on a rope) emblazoned with my favorite Marvel character, Spider-Man. Astonishingly, just over five decades later, this scenario still plays out in many homes. According to a 2021 survey by the National Retail Federation, the next generation of young kids are feeling *the pull* like I did, with superhero costumes nabbing five of the top ten Halloween costume spots. Sitting atop that list is your friendly neighborhood Spider-Man from the MCU.[2] But what about adults? As of the time of writing, we see an even more revealing phenomenon at the box office: adults plunking down big dollars to experience the MCU's latest offerings. Men, the assumed demographic, are only a "click" (or statistically marginal percentage) ahead of women in viewership attached to the MCU in both the "avid" and "casual" fan categories.[3]

Kids. Adults. Male. Female. Everyone feels *the pull*.

While the secret sauce of the MCU's success is hotly debated within its global "fanverse," the following common denominators go a long way to explaining *the attachment* we feel toward the characters and overarching story being told:

- Characters with personal backstories and shortcomings
- Transforming encounters or traumas that redefine their purpose

- Special and potentially dangerous powers or skill sets in their possession
- The execution of justice
- Sacrificial actions taken for the sake of others
- Confrontation of evil forces that threaten humanity
- Purposes and missions that are bigger than themselves
- Willingness, in specific spaces and times, to risk their legacy
- Humor in the midst of super problems, super chaos, and superheroes

These themes have a mysterious and strong touch point in the human soul. The critical thing the MCU lacks is a basis for fans to experience these longings themselves. The world has paid billions to *vicariously* experience them while viewing the films.

Each film is a synthetic tease that exploits an authentic and supernatural reality.

God has made everything beautiful for its own time. He has planted eternity in the human heart, but even so, people cannot see the whole scope of God's work from beginning to end.[4]

God. Eternity. Reality. The overarching tale to which we *actually* belong.

Eternity is God's realm outside of space and time that has, through Jesus alone, broken into our space and into our times to call on the souls of men and women for the greatness we crave inside. While on earth, Jesus called this breakthrough and advent among people the Kingdom of God—the dimension where his super-humanness and super-story connects us with eternity. He declared that it was here *now*. He declared its power and active presence. He pointed to its signature activities and core agenda among us. He pointed out its evil adversary. But most importantly for our purposes here, he called all those who believe in him to proactively advance it. Why? Because it is the dimension where all believers in Christ are intended to work out their unique stories. It is the source of the pull we feel inside that cannot be satisfied by self-destructive rip-off versions. It is the hole in the soul, the ultimate reality we seek. It is *the pull* inside that leads to our strongest legacy—where we are called specifically and uniquely to be great and do great things.

It is God's endgame in which *all believers* in Christ . . .

- Bring their personal backstories *and* shortcomings.
- Experience a transforming encounter that redefines their purpose.
- Are empowered by the Holy Spirit and made dangerous for goodness.
- Are used to bring God's love and justice.
- Sacrifice in their context, like Jesus, for the sake of others.
- Confront and defeat evil forces/agendas in the power of the Holy Spirit.
- Engage in missions reflecting Kingdom purposes that are bigger than self.
- Risk for God's glory and eternal legacy in their "moment in time" on earth.
- Laugh along the way, perplexed and amused at how God works.

Now that he has you, this is where *he is taking you.*

Whoever believes in me will do the works I have been doing, and they will do even greater things than these, because I am going to the Father.[5]

Did you catch that? Whoever believes . . . *will do.*

Feel the pull. Start getting excited. Sense where this is leading. Your beliefs set you up for supernatural action.

Transformed to Overflow

I love Bolognese sauce with tagliatelle pasta.

Eating my favorite pasta dish, however, is preceded by a process.

- Regular water is placed into a pot.
- A fire is lit, and the pot is positioned on top of the flame.
- Time passes, and the water heated by the fire produces steam as little bubbles.
- More time passes, more steam is created, and the little bubbles get bigger.
- More time passes, and the surface of the water starts moving as steam bubbles rise up through the water and break free.
- More time passes, and all the water in the pot is moving with waves of fast-moving bubbles, causing a full boil.
- The pasta is added to the boiling water and cooks for seven minutes.
- The hot water is drained from the now-cooked pasta.
- I smother the pasta in my beef and pork Bolognese and enjoy the product of my labor. Yum!

Water. Fire. Time. Steam. Release. Yum.

Every day, in homes and restaurants around the world, this ritual is repeated perhaps a billion times. You have done it. You might be doing it right now. Physics of Cooking 101. Water—the object of change. Fire—the agent of change. Time—allows for the process of change. Steam—produced by the change.

Release—something is allowed to move freely after previously being contained. In this case, it's the power of the steam. Yum—the pleasure of eating and experiencing the purpose of the process. No transformation of the water, no yum!

Basic cooking physics mirrors basic spiritual physics, a point that is going to be important for this journey. Break down the physics and we start to see a process, or journey, that God wants to reproduce with every believer, leading to his specific, experiential outcome. You, like water, are the object of change. The Holy Spirit, like fire, is the agent of change applied and deposited in you. Time and cooperation with the Holy Spirit, like heat applied to water over time, triggers the process of spiritual transformation. Christlike character within, like steam, is produced by the change. Christlike conduct, like steam breaking the surface into a boil, moves freely and visibly *out of us* into our world. Conduct is the natural expression of character. Kingdom influence and impact, like tasting and experiencing a finished dish, is the gratifying sensation we seek as believers—and God's ultimate goal for our personal spiritual process.

God's intentional process always fulfills his Kingdom purpose.

Christ followers are transformed by the Holy Spirit to overflow *in their contexts*. Your context includes the people and the places uniquely connected to your life and everyday rhythms right now. The Holy Spirit's *work in you* (God's intentional process) is supernaturally intended to become a visible *work through you* (God's Kingdom purpose) in your unique time, your specific spaces, your relationships, and your cultural context. While personal transformation is part of God's process within us, it is never the only goal he has for individuals who belong to his super-story. His vision—through the person and work of the Holy Spirit in us—is a worldwide overflow of Kingdom power *into* a dark, dying, and desperate world that is battling evil and injustice.

Holy Spirit transformation always leads to Holy Spirit overflow.

Jesus stood and said in a loud voice, "Let anyone who is
thirsty come to me and drink. Whoever believes in me,
as Scripture has said, rivers of living water will flow from
within them." By this he meant the Spirit, whom those
who believed in him were later to receive. Up to that time
the Spirit had not been given, since Jesus had not yet
been glorified.[6]

"You will receive power when the Holy Spirit comes on
you; and you will be my witnesses in Jerusalem, and in all
Judea and Samaria, and to the ends of the earth."[7]

Follow the process and arc of experiencing the Holy Spirit.

- Jesus is prophesying the Holy Spirit *filling* us.
- Jesus is prophesying the Holy Spirit's *transforming* us
  within.
- Jesus is prophesying the Holy Spirit's *overflowing* out of us
  into the world in which we live.

Anyone who misses the arc that Jesus foretells will miss God's
fullest intention for life—the great adventure of the soul for which
we were created. Jesus was no stranger to the tendencies of men
and the inner battles they would experience trying to let go of the
synthetic cultural expressions of masculine or personal greatness.
This is why he addressed the inner tension and challenge head-on.

Then, calling the crowd to join his disciples, he said, "If
any of you wants to be my follower, you must give up
your own way, take up your cross, and follow me. If you

try to hang on to your life, you will lose it. But if you give up your life for my sake and for the sake of the Good News, you will save it. And what do you benefit if you gain the whole world but lose your own soul? Is anything worth more than your soul?"[8]

We can hang on to man's purposes or let go in order to advance God's purposes.

For every pull of God, there is an opposite and forceful pull by culture. For every authentic and ultimate moment of eternal influence, there is a synthetic and immediate moment available for carnal indulgence. For every greater work of the Holy Spirit in and through us, there is available a lesser work of selfish impulses in us and through us. For every moment of Christ-inspired sacrifice for others, there springs up the comforting rationalization that it is not our problem. For every call of Christ to risk Kingdom advancement in faith, there is a suggestion by the devil that attempts to thwart it by stoking a fear.

The pull. The tension. The choice.

The journey you choose will flow most directly from the strength of your inner transformation at this point in your relationship with God. Specifically, it will flow from your sense of identity in Christ and your security in God's love. These were the exact journeys we took in *Dangerous Good: The Coming Revolution of Men Who Care* and *Failsafe: Living Secure in God's Acceptance*. You may be tracking right into this final book of the trilogy while others are starting at the end of it. (That works too!)

Whatever your journey, God has this book in your hands right now because his Spirit in you is calling. In your soul, you feel the pull to be dangerous with goodness. The power to actually live that out is emanating from knowing who you are in Christ, being fully accepted by him, fully loved by him, and fully defined by him. You know God's highest vision and noblest goal for you is Christlikeness. His love has freed you from fear in order to pursue his character. Your failsafe—God's love—is in place. Your soul is secure, and your gaze is fixed.

No matter what happens to you, no matter what mountains you have to climb, and no matter what the personal cost, what Jesus foretold about your outward trajectory into the world will be manifested in this hour and in your personal context. You see the horizon of your life and know it is time to elevate your influence for Christ and risk more for him. Your comfort is solid, knowing that God's Spirit and God's Word will not fail to complete the inner transformation that will lead to the greater works of Jesus through your life. This season of overflow will influence many, and you will join millions of other brothers in Christ right now in a worldwide shift to overflow, influence, and impact for Christ in these last days.

Identity and inner security in Christ's love leads to Holy Spirit explosivity.

As you read each chapter, you will be challenged to live out what God has poured into your spirit in real time—that hour, that day, or that week. Your growing sense of identity in him will widen your availability to him, which will activate more influence for him. Release of the Holy Spirit's power will come about supernaturally. God will actually bring people to you in natural ways in order for you to be used in supernatural ways you could not have imagined.

Expect filling. Prepare for overflow. Loose the spread.

fill (v.): to put into as much as can be held; to supply with a full complement; to cause to swell[9]

The disciples, seeing the Master with their own eyes, were awestruck. Jesus repeated his greeting: "Peace to you. Just as the Father sent me, I send you."

Then he took a deep breath and breathed into them. "Receive the Holy Spirit," he said.[10]

overflow (v.): to fill a space to capacity and spread beyond its limits[11]

They couldn't take their eyes off them—Peter and John standing there so confident, so sure of themselves! The fascination of the religious leaders deepened when they realized these two were laymen with no training in Scripture or formal education. They recognized them as companions of Jesus, but with the man right before them, seeing him standing there so upright—so healed!—what could they say against that?

They sent them out of the room so they could work out a plan. They talked it over: "What can we do with these men? By now it's known all over town that a miracle has occurred, and that they are behind it. There is no way we can refute that."[12]

spread (v.): to open or expand over a larger area; to extend the range or incidence of; to make widely known[13]

And with that, the apostles were on their way, continuing to witness and spread the Message of God's salvation, preaching in every Samaritan town they passed through on their return to Jerusalem.[14]

Keep in step. This is where everything has been leading.

For the anxious longing of the creation waits eagerly for the revealing of the sons of God.[15]

Holy Spirit,

Thank you for dwelling in me. Thank you for sealing my identity. Thank you for conforming me to the image of Christ. Thank you for filling me and controlling me. Thank you for manifesting the fruit of the Spirit and gifts of the Spirit in me. Thank you for being the fire of God in me, transforming me in my inner man, giving me the very character of Christ. Thank you for securing my spirit through God's love and acceptance, setting me free from condemnation and comparison. Holy Spirit, in the name of Jesus, I surrender to your overflow from me and into the spaces, places, and people you have assigned to my life. I want the greater works of Christ manifested in me and through me right now, according to your Word and promise. Align my spirit, my energy, and my body with your Kingdom super-story. Holy Spirit, use me today. Open my eyes to the Kingdom of God and the exact part I am playing in it. Open new doors and help me to step through them in Jesus' name and for your pleasure. Amen.

This is the confidence we have in approaching God: that if we ask anything according to his will, he hears us. And if we know that he hears us—whatever we ask—we know that we have what we asked of him.[16]

PART I

OVERFLOWING IDENTITY

1

SALT BY CONTACT

I Am in the Mix

"MY WIFE CRASHED ON THE OPERATING TABLE."

This was the second time I had seen Ryan at our gym. He was not a part of my plan that day as we both waited to get inside for the next class. I know that seems selfish. But these sixty-minute sessions of high-intensity interval training are the spaces in my week that detoxify my spirit. I am not super chatty when I go, but on this day, I asked a total stranger how he was doing. His words about events in recent weeks landed with a weight that only vulnerability plus unvarnished reality can possess.

The only proper response was, "I am so sorry."

The good news was that this event was not the end of the story. Apparently, a routine procedure turned into a sepsis infection, which turned into the body shutting down, which turned into the heart *restarting*—all in one medical event. While his wife remembered none of it, Ryan lived through all of it—all the emotions, the horrible thoughts, and the uncertainty that came with being minutes from losing the light of his life. And there I was, unsuspectingly strolling through the door of the gym, asking a normal question, and getting drawn into a major life event. Naturally, my wheels were spinning as Ryan relayed the awful experience of knowing his wife almost died on the operating table and then the relief of her heart starting back up and her pulling out of the infection and coma over the course of the next few days.

No coincidences here. Ryan booked the same workout I did on this day, at this time, as a first step toward resuming his life after such a traumatic and unwelcome interruption.

Clearly, he needed to talk about this with someone, and we did talk for about ten minutes before our workout started and then again in class between rowing and weights. Since his wife was out of the woods and recovering well, the big need I could sense was a friendly outlet to process his emotions. But having been let into the heart of someone's life, I was now praying this meeting would lead to a friendship and ongoing conversation. In short order, my prayer was answered as I learned I would be seeing Ryan every other day. His restarted workout schedule looked identical to mine.

We exchanged numbers. But it gets better.

After meeting me in the morning, Ryan went home, showered, and went to the fine jewelry department at Nordstrom, during the mid-shift, to bay number one, where his wife's favorite brand of jewelry resides behind the glass. He had it in his mind to purchase a get-well-please-don't-ever-die-suddenly-again present to express his love for her and celebrate life.

My wife, Chrissy, works in the fine jewelry department at Nordstrom. She works the mid-shift, and she is the specialist for Ryan's wife's favorite brand. She was standing in bay one to greet Ryan, totally unaware that I had just met Ryan earlier that morning. In her customary way, Chrissy engaged Ryan warmly: "Is this for a special occasion?" As Chrissy talked with Ryan, he was able to relay to another friendly ear the ordeal he had been through the past couple of weeks. After hearing Ryan's story, Chrissy helped him pick out the perfect bracelet for his wife.

As our individual workdays were winding up, Chrissy and I texted, making dinner plans and looking forward to a debrief. Since you have the backstory, you can see what's coming—an epic collision of providence in real space and time for the sake of a real person who is the object of God's real concern. They say ignorance is bliss. Well, in this case, our ignorance of the other's encounter with the same person was the context of a supernatural revelation. It sounded like this:

Me: *How was Nordy today?*

Chrissy: *Good. I had this customer whose wife's heart stopped during a surgery, but they revived her and she lived! I helped the husband pick out a bracelet to buy her.*

Me: *Wait! Are you being serious right now?*

Chrissy: *Totally. She went in for a routine procedure, got sepsis, and crashed on the operating table.*

Me: *Was this customer tall?*

Chrissy *(head tilting)*: *Yes.*

Me: *Did he have a beard?*

Chrissy *(hesitatingly)*: *Yeeeeeessss.*

Me: *Was his name Ryan?*

Chrissy: *Yes! How did you know that?*

Me: *You are not going to believe this. God is on the move.*

I can't quite describe the feeling we had in that moment. How do you process an encounter with divine providence that is so in your face like that? No mystery to it at all!

The idea that our individual stories actively intersect with God's great super-story and his concern for every person demands reflection, inspires awe, sparks wonder, and produces a serious "Whoa!" But more importantly, it should amplify for us the supernatural purposes of the spaces we occupy and the people who are in them. God has sovereignly and strategically placed us in the mix of specific cultures and communities to execute his plan with people in the rhythms and routines of everyday life.

Jesus said this would be the case for every follower.

Let me tell you why you are here. You're here to be salt-seasoning that brings out the God-flavors of this earth.[1]

Salt Is Everywhere

In so many ways—salt shows up. Everywhere. Every day.

Chances are that within the last few hours you have interacted with salt by choice or by its simple presence in so many things. From prescriptions to plastics, leather goods to lavender soaps, paper to pottery, salt is a key manufacturing ingredient. It is also the silent staple, sitting on billions of tables in homes, cafés, and restaurants worldwide, largely unnoticed but essential to have in the mix if food is being served. In fact, most cultures divide the totality of daily meals into two categories—sweet and salty—choosing salt to represent the savory side of the menu. But you can't limit salt to the kitchen alone. During the winter months in many states, it is spread across snow-filled roads and walkways. Physiologically, the body uses salt to absorb and transport nutrients, maintain blood pressure and the right balance of fluid, transmit nerve signals, and contract and relax muscles.[2] You *literally* can't escape it! Salt is critical to a body's health. And lastly, our little blue planet orbiting the sun appears blue from outer space because salt water, holding trillions of tons of salt, covers almost three-quarters of its surface.

Ordinary. Everywhere. A variety of purposes.

Jesus declared us "salt." He chose this working illustration for our identity and commission because it resonated in his world, in his context. Then, like now, salt was ordinary, everywhere, and used for a variety of purposes. But in the ancient Near Eastern mindset, salt also had some specific purposes that are not so familiar to us, and we need to explore them if we are to understand his commission to overflow in our world. So how would someone who just decided to follow Jesus interpret being called "salt-seasoning that brings out the God-flavors of this earth"?

You make things better by contact.

This is no surprise at all. Taste-wise, salt makes just about everything better on contact. It is added to flavorless food to give it life. It is added to food that already has flavor to further draw out that flavor. Salt is added to provide a contrast. As a parallel, God adds us into families, churches, communities, workplaces, and social environments to add Holy Spirit presence, make supernatural contact, and influence those around us for these same purposes. We are placed or sent into specific spaces to bring the life of the Kingdom where it has not yet taken hold, to draw out and magnify blessings already present, and to be distinctly different in a

Spirit-empowered way by making contact with those people in those environments.

Think about your purpose this way: God has you available to him. He can add you into the mix of situations and relationships directly connected to the people and places you frequent. More specifically, he can add your character in Christ, your conduct that is an expression of that character, your insight and wisdom rooted in his truth, your prayers, your spiritual gifts, and your direct testimony of God's presence in your life. All of these enhance the quality of the environments you are assigned by God to enter, drawing out their potential for Kingdom purposes. Just by being aware that you are intentionally added by God into *all* the environments you presently occupy infuses you with one specific aim as salt—*make them better by contact.*

The Holy Spirit's mission *in you* is to make you better—more like Christ in your character. He improves you. He increases righteousness. He secures you in God's love. He grows your awareness of his love and your ability to love others the way he has loved you.

The Holy Spirit's mission *through you* is the same, but now *you are the one* improving specific spaces and places, situations and settings, connections and communities.

This is what Jesus had in mind with his "just as I" statements connected to loving, forgiving, and being merciful in the Gospels. It's also what Paul had in mind when he coached believers to "season" their interactions with people, making those encounters *better.*

> Let your conversation be always full of grace, seasoned
> with salt, so that you may know how to answer everyone.[3]

Notice what the nature of the believers' Holy Spirit overflow is? Grace.

You are salt by contact, and upon contact with you, people

experience favor, blessing, and a response from you that is either uncalled for, undeserved, or unmerited. Grace. It shocks and most likely will offend all sense of fairness. Grace. There is no rationale for it—it just comes. Grace. It is a kindness overflowing from God through you that demands no reciprocity and no returning of the favor. Grace. It feels unusual to people and is mysteriously attractive.

Grace is the opposite of unkindness, abuse, cruelty, harshness, evil, nastiness, self-importance, and coldheartedness. Jesus said, "Freely you have received; freely give."[4]

God says: "Overflow grace in the power of the Holy Spirit on contact."

That's what happened when Jesus made contact with us.

But the gift is not like the trespass. For if the many died
by the trespass of the one man, how much more did
God's grace and the gift that came by the grace of the one
man, Jesus Christ, overflow to the many![5]

Now—having experienced that as one of the "many"—guess what happens when we make contact with others God has placed in our lives.

We're not keeping this quiet, not on your life. Just like
the psalmist who wrote, "I believed it, so I said it," we
say what we believe. And what we believe is that the
One who raised up the Master Jesus will just as certainly
raise us up with you, alive. Every detail works to your
advantage and to God's glory: more and more grace, more
and more people, more and more praise![6]

God does not make mistakes. He is present in the details. He has set things up so that you are in a position to salt the people you meet and the environments you are in with something different, something supernatural, something mysterious, and something wonderful.

Grace.

You preserve goodness and prevent corruption.

In Jesus' day, salt was like refrigeration is today. Rub salt into meat and fish, and you could stop it from decaying so that it remained edible for a long time. The special property? Salt draws bacteria-producing moisture out of foods, drying them and making it possible to store food for extended periods. So when a follower of Jesus heard the identity statement, "You are salt," many filtered it culturally in a couple of ways. First, they understood just how valuable salt was to their daily existence. Second, they knew salt had a special power to preserve food and prevent spoiling. Salt in the first century was so valuable that it was used as currency. And just like you have to restrict the printing of money to create controls in a large economy, governments in Jesus' day had to legally manage, monitor, and restrict salt production. Roman soldiers sometimes received their pay in salt, which is the origin of the word *salary*.[7]

Think about your specific purpose in the world for the Kingdom of God in this way: you are a highly valued, super-useful, powerful stopper of corruption in your community. You might even want to reread that in the first person, saying "I am" instead of "You are." Think about it. You are the currency of his Kingdom. God rewards others in your life by giving you to them as "salary," which they can rely on to help them function and make progress. You ensure that the Kingdom realm works smoothly as you (the valuable salt) submit to God's oversight, control, and distribution of your energies.

So let's reset that.

As God's salt, we preserve and protect, specifically preserving the good and protecting against the corrupting forces of godless culture, the depraved impulses of men, and the devil himself. This is what Jesus had in mind when he commissioned his followers to enter the mixes of people and places connected uniquely to them and said:

Be preservatives yourselves. Preserve the peace.[8]

Notice what the Holy Spirit overflow is? Peace. God's *shalom*.

Upon contact with you, people experience more peace and less chaos because of the presence of God through the Holy Spirit in you! To be clear, God's peace is not just the absence of conflict—it is God's "salt" in the mix, taking action to restore a broken situation, a broken relationship, or a broken heart. When things are fragmented, God's man ties things together as a whole and sets it as one again. This ability is an overflow of God's presence in you spilling over into the work, social, and family networks you belong to—new and old, professional and personal.

As you enter the home, give it your greeting. If the home is deserving, let your peace rest on it; if it is not, let your peace return to you.[9]

You're blessed when you can show people how to cooperate instead of compete or fight. That's when you discover who you really are, and your place in God's family.[10]

The Holy Spirit has specific work to do in the places and with the people assigned to you. He has chosen to sprinkle you into the variety of settings in which you currently reside in order to help people experience peace with God, peace with others, and peace within, no matter what chaos and confusion surround. Sometimes, you being salty looks like doing good, and in doing good, the chaos and panic caused by evil are eliminated. Other times, your very presence acts like a preservative preventing situational, relational, or emotional decay—you are literally a peacemaker through presence. You can also seek peace by pursuing and securing agreement, offering or fostering forgiveness that leads to restoration, or simply celebrating truth in a situation, which always leads to greater peace. Salty people pursue peace wherever God puts them.

> Whoever wants to embrace life and see the day fill
> up with good, here's what you do: say nothing evil or
> hurtful; snub evil and cultivate good; run after peace for
> all you're worth. God looks on all this with approval,
> listening and responding well to what he's asked; but he
> turns his back on those who do evil things.[11]

> God says: "Overflow peace in the power of the Holy Spirit."
> You preserve good. You protect peace.
> Salt is not just savory. It saves.

You make sacrifices in order to please God.

In Jesus' culture, people would certainly have thought of seasoning and preserving, but a few who heard themselves being compared to salt might have remembered a scriptural connection—thinking about Moses, about worship, about their covenant relationship, and about the right way to offer sacrifices pleasing to God.

> Season every presentation of your Grain-Offering with
> salt. Don't leave the salt of the covenant with your God
> out of your Grain-Offerings. Present all your offerings
> with salt.[12]

Abijah took a prominent position on Mount Zemaraim in the hill country of Ephraim and gave this speech: "Listen, Jeroboam and all Israel! Don't you realize that GOD, the one and only God of Israel, established David and his sons as the permanent rulers of Israel, ratified by a 'covenant of salt'—GOD's kingdom ruled by GOD's king?"[13]

Salt has a long history of reflecting a binding agreement between two parties, and when applied to agreements between God and man, it carries specific meaning. Thus King Abijah of Judah in the passage above flexes this awareness and refers to the strong, legally binding promise of God to give Israel to David and his sons forever. How? By referring to the salt covenant between God and his people.

Many who heard Jesus refer to his followers as "salt" could easily connect that illustration directly to their relationship with God and what it meant for them. Most immediately, it meant the keeping of promises—promises made by God to his people and promises made by his people to him. The covenant of salt included loyalty, honesty, and a lasting relationship. In biblical times, all Jewish listeners understood that the covenant of salt meant that they would keep their word at all costs. Fast-forward to Middle Eastern people groups today, and you will still hear the phrase: "There is salt between us," meaning the two parties are keeping the commitment made to each other. The public claim of identity in God only had integrity if there was public commitment and conduct to back it up. In fact, this concept of keeping your word in your relationship with God (and being willing to sacrifice for it) can be seen in an actual "come to Jesus" moment in the Gospels. A frustrated Jesus exclaims to his so-called followers:

Why do you call me, "Lord, Lord," and do not do what
I say?[14]

Ouch! The personal claim of connection is meaningless to
Jesus without visible conduct that reflects the relationship—a
relationship not only in name but also in daily commitment, daily
obedience, and sealed through daily *sacrifice* in light of one's commitment. The "salt" of public sacrifice for the sake of relationship
is Jesus' own example, is the core identity of the believer, and is
at the center of our motivation to keep our commitment to Jesus
publicly at any cost.

God says: "Overflow your sacrificial love for me in the power
of the Holy Spirit."

We ask: "Why do you want that, Father?"

God says: "Because there is salt between us."

Greater love has no one than this: to lay down one's life
for one's friends. You are my friends if you do what I
command.[15]

I identified myself completely with him. Indeed, I have
been crucified with Christ. My ego is no longer central. It
is no longer important that I appear righteous before you
or have your good opinion, and I am no longer driven
to impress God. Christ lives in me. The life you see me
living is not "mine," but it is lived by faith in the Son of
God, who loved me and gave himself for me. I am not
going to go back on that.[16]

He died for everyone so that those who receive his new
life will no longer live for themselves. Instead, they will
live for Christ, who died and was raised for them.[17]

His example. Our identity. Our energy overflowing in sacrificial commitment.

The salt of our covenant is sacrifice, and it shows.

You judge evil and confront injustice.

This may surprise you, but there are more references to salt being used in judgment than for any other purpose.

- Lot's wife was turned into a pillar of salt.[18]
- Moses warned the Israelites that the consequence of breaking covenant with God—forgetting they were his people and instead worshiping other gods—would be their land becoming "a fire-blackened wasteland of brimstone and salt flats."[19]
- Gideon's son Abimelech razed a city of rebels by "[sowing] it with salt."[20]

When Jesus compared his followers to salt, I imagine there were more than a few who took a deep breath because, in his time and culture, salt was used to express judgment upon evil.

As we have learned, all Spirit-empowered believers are living out a personal story in the shared place of God's super-story called the Kingdom of God. In that Kingdom—his supernatural universe—an epic battle between good and evil is being waged. When you think about being "salt" that judges evil and confronts injustice, it makes perfect sense from God's perspective. He scatters his "salty ones" into billions of spaces every day, all over the world, as a way of judging evil; destroying wickedness; diluting lust, greed, and murder; and preventing injustice from taking root. We are his boots on the ground against evil, which exists and advances right alongside good and God. God's "salt of the earth" need to be mindful that they serve a God and King who feels strongly about very specific things and is proactive in advancing what he is for while thwarting, judging, and ultimately, destroying what he is against.

> The LORD loves righteousness and justice.[21]

> For the eyes of the Lord are on the righteous and his ears are attentive to their prayer, but the face of the Lord is against those who do evil.[22]

> And I tell you that you are Peter, and on this rock I will build my church, and the gates of Hades will not overcome it. I will give you the keys of the kingdom of heaven; whatever you bind on earth will be bound in heaven, and whatever you loose on earth will be loosed in heaven.[23]

He loves "righteousness and justice." He is against "those who do evil." And he has a new community called the church that is an evil-defeating machine.

The very existence of Christ followers who comprise the church is the supernatural and living expression of God's position on earth against all evil, all unrighteousness, and all injustice. He is actively judging and confronting evil now, deputizing us with his power and authority to confront, overpower, and overcome evil as we encounter it in the contexts of our lives and the culture we live in. The ones who are taught to pray, "lead us not into temptation, but deliver us from evil"[24] are also the ones who are filled with the Spirit of God to destroy all enemies aligned against God within and without. Just like Jesus.

> Dear children, do not let anyone lead you astray. The one who does what is right is righteous, just as he is righteous.

The one who does what is sinful is of the devil, because
the devil has been sinning from the beginning. The reason
the Son of God appeared was to destroy the devil's work.[25]

Did you catch that? The reason Jesus came to earth? To destroy
what the devil is doing. We ask: "What the devil is going on?" and
mean it—literally. We are the salt that confronts evil. Christ's own
mission on earth is the best indicator of what ours should be. But
before we run to battle, he advises running to the mirror.

Jesus' strongest and most graphic exhortation of judgment suggests that we begin our campaign against the sin and evil residing
in our own lives and in the house of God.

If your hand causes you to stumble, cut it off. It is better for
you to enter life maimed than with two hands to go into
hell, where the fire never goes out. And if your foot causes
you to stumble, cut it off. It is better for you to enter life
crippled than to have two feet and be thrown into hell. And
if your eye causes you to stumble, pluck it out. It is better for
you to enter the kingdom of God with one eye than to have
two eyes and be thrown into hell, where "the worms that eat
them do not die, and the fire is not quenched." Everyone
will be salted with fire.

Salt is good, but if it loses its saltiness, how can you
make it salty again?[26]

We are the "salt of the earth"[27]—the ones who confront evil,
beginning with ourselves.

- "Salt"—the agent of judgment and testing—recognizes sin.
  Note the language of "If your hand causes you to stumble
  . . . if your foot causes you to stumble . . . if your eye causes

you to stumble." Jesus assumed we know our own patterns of weakness and ritual failure and commanded his followers (hyperbolically) to take drastic measures in eliminating them from their lives. This isn't nickel poker. The stakes are much higher.

- "Salting"—the action of judgment—amputates sin. Amputation in Jesus' day did not involve an anesthesiologist. It was painful. It was thorough. It was worthwhile, because it meant that the threat of infection was eliminated. The pain of self-confrontation is worth the prize of present power and eternal life.

- "Saltiness"—the active power of the salty ones to influence—is destroyed when sin is not confronted in a believer.

Salt is stable. Salt lasts. Salt has many uses. Salt is everywhere. *But* salt can be rendered useless.

The Big *But*

But. It's a small word that carries a lot of power. When we use the word *but*, people brace themselves for what comes next, or they might even make a face. We may not want hear what follows it, but we have to pay attention if we want a complete picture. We have to listen to resolve our feelings and prepare to act in response to what the *whole truth* is. When Jesus uses the word *but* as he talks about our identity and calling to be salt, it is only reasonable to lean in and pay super close attention.

You are the salt of the earth. But if the salt loses its saltiness, how can it be made salty again? It is no longer good for anything, except to be thrown out and trampled underfoot.[28]

Salt has a kryptonite—a neutralizer that renders something formerly powerful *powerless* to advance God's agenda in the world.

Salt in Jesus' day was derived from salt marshes, and it contained impurities that had to be "leached," or filtered out. This was possible because pure salt was more soluble than the impurities and could be separated. This process would leave a residue so diluted and impure it was of little practical worth. Things that are "thrown out" or "trampled underfoot" are things that have no practical value. So was Jesus saying that the "salt of the earth," which is so valuable in the Kingdom of God, could, through a process of impurity, become worthless and useless?

Yes. Here's how.

If the world hates you, keep in mind that it hated me
first. If you belonged to the world, it would love you as
its own. As it is, you do not belong to the world, but I
have chosen you out of the world. That is why the world
hates you.[29]

Jesus told his men they were chosen "out of the world"—the polluting factor. His point? Worldliness and godliness are at odds. We can be salt that remains salty and useful, or we can be a diluted residue worth nothing. We can be pure, or we can be polluted. We can allow God's Spirit and Word to wash and leach out the world's ways from our spirits, or we can blend the world's ways with God's ways at our own peril. It is an everyday choice to have spiritual boundaries to preserve our saltiness.

Make no mistake: God's intention is for every believer to have a positive Kingdom effect, but he does not shield us from potential pollution of our commitment. He didn't shield Jesus in the wilderness encounter, where Satan, appealing to Jesus' flesh, offered him bread and tempted him to break his fast. Satan has not changed. The battle has not changed. The offer has not changed. The path to victory and staying pure before God has not changed either.

> The devil led him up to a high place and showed him in an instant all the kingdoms of the world. And he said to him, "I will give you all their authority and splendor; it has been given to me, and I can give it to anyone I want to. If you worship me, it will all be yours."
>
> Jesus answered, "It is written: 'Worship the Lord your God and serve him only.'"[30]

Full of the Holy Spirit. Led by the Spirit. Speaking words of the Spirit. The result?

> When the devil had finished all this tempting, he left him until an opportune time.[31]

Jesus did not let worldliness pollute his godliness. Two more times the devil came to Jesus to solicit compromise and pollute his commitment. Two more offers to be worldly that matched the moment. But the same Holy Spirit's filling and leading led to the same plunging of God's Word into the heart of each suggestion. The devil left him. The Son of God showed all future sons of God who are commissioned to be the salt of God how to stay salty (uncompromised) and remain unpolluted (pure). What Jesus models for us is meant for us.

Saltiness is keeping all your Holy Spirit capacity to influence. Saltiness requires being full of and led by the Holy Spirit every day. Saltiness requires speaking words of the Spirit as a way of life.

God says: "Stay filled. Stay close. Stay ready to speak truth. Stay pure."

Stay salty.

Holy Spirit,

I want to be used by you in the mix of my life. I declare in Jesus' name the fulfillment of your purposes in me and through me in the spaces where you have placed me. You are my helper and my guide. You make me salty. Show me where and how I can make things better for your glory. Use me to bring life where there is no life in you. Use me to draw out blessings that are present but unseen. Use me to provide a holy and healthy contrast to the world.

Holy Spirit, overflow your radical and mysterious grace through me and give me courage to express it. Overflow your peace through me as you lead me to do good and protect peace. Overflow your authority through me and help me to recognize and confront evil agendas, defeating them with the spiritual weapons of your presence in me, your power through me, and your Word coming out of me. Fill me. Lead me. Let your Word come to mind so I may meet the tempter's suggestions head-on and thwart his plans.

Holy Spirit, keep me free of worldliness and from blending culture's ways with your ways. I ask that you keep sprinkling me into whatever situations and places you need me to serve the Kingdom. Keep me salty today and every day until I am with you forever. In Jesus' name I pray. Amen.

2

LIGHT BY CONTRAST

I Am Visible

IT WAS SO COUNTERCULTURAL, the tension in the room was sliceable.

Our men's team in Haiti is always ready for the unexpected. We have gone every year for the past eleven years, endeavoring to make heroes of Haitians, to serve the least of these, and to minister to a next generation of leaders. Children abandoned by their parents to the streets have found our shelters, a family, an education, and Jesus. Villages get regular visits and supplies of food. Pastors are encouraged and trained. Churches are planted. Communities are transformed. We just keep coming. Brick by cement brick, trip after trip, and team after team have established a pattern of consistency that fosters trust and makes our gospel message authentic.

My close staff comrades, Rick and Dave, have been the drivers of the vision for community development in Haiti, while the men of Crossline Church have provided the muscle and resources needed to realize many of their visions. These trips are wild and woolly. They boil your blood and break your heart. They leave you exhausted and energized at the same time.

Twenty-plus guys doing truly different, truly good things with their vacation time—it's a head scratcher. All of the men filing out of the back of the "tap-tap" (a converted flatbed truck with a steel roof and benches) have left their families and traveled more than three thousand miles because God has sent them to bring one message: you are loved by God and by me. These guys accumulate seven layers of grime and sweat each day for the opportunity to live that message out and obey Jesus' command—and they find it addicting.

This particular morning, however, we were doing something new. We exited the tap-tap and entered a room *full of women*.

This is a men's trip. We are very careful and work hard never to compromise cultural or moral boundaries. The difference here is that these women serve in our children's shelter, and our team leader on the ground (Rick) heard directly from the Holy Spirit the night before that the men (Haitian and American) were to bless and serve these women by washing their feet and praying over them. We were not total strangers, and this moment was planned and agreed to by the staff women. No one was required to be there; they wanted to be there. But a cultural tension was present. In Haiti, women serve the men, not the opposite. In fact, broken male culture in Haiti fosters so much injustice for women and children, it rises to the level of the demonic and makes me physically shake with anger. It is embedded in Haitian culture and largely accepted, and women seem resigned to it. So while our track record as a men's team goes a long way, all the trauma rooted in the character and conduct of men might have caused the women to view us through a lens of mistrust, cynicism, and pain.

Also present was the obvious interpersonal tension of foot washing. Talk about up close, personal, and intimate! Think about it: Who has touched your feet recently outside of a salon environment? It would be strange enough to have a nonprofessional touch your feet, much less a perfect stranger who has been directed by God to touch them.

The final tension was spiritual. The Holy Spirit told us to serve forty Haitian women by washing their feet, learning their names, and praying God's healing and blessing over them. We did this one-on-one, with a translator repeating our blessing in Creole so the women could not just experience our concern but also hear our words of concern in their own language. I imagine the devil didn't appreciate that men were blessing and serving women instead of harming and using them. It was a moment when fears and lies were conquered by humility and faith in Christ. Like I said, the tension *was* sliceable.

This experience reminded me what God calls us to:

> If you try to hang on to your life, you will lose it. But if you give up your life for my sake and for the sake of the Good News, you will save it.[1]

The moment the first man began the process of foot washing and the woman on the other end of the gesture received it, all present tensions suddenly gave way to the dominating peace and presence of the Holy Spirit at work. Picture this:

- Men gently and carefully washing the ankles and feet of women
- Women safely receiving this act from men with appreciation and understanding
- Men weeping for reasons known only to God as they humbled themselves
- Strong women letting their guard down and allowing their own tears to flow

- Prayers in English being spoken and felt
- Prayers in Creole being spoken and felt
- Dozens of children living in the shelter watching this sacred moment
- Haitian men serving Haitian women
- Awe, wonder, and swishing water
- Gentle drying
- Closed eyes and raised hands
- Inner healings and deliverances
- Brothers and sisters caring for one another

So much tension. So much contrast. So much Holy Spirit breakthrough.

When one of the Pharisees invited Jesus to have dinner with him, he went to the Pharisee's house and reclined at the table. A woman in that town who lived a sinful life learned that Jesus was eating at the Pharisee's house, so she came there with an alabaster jar of perfume. As she stood behind him at his feet weeping, she began to wet his feet with her tears. Then she wiped them with her hair, kissed them and poured perfume on them.

When the Pharisee who had invited him saw this, he said to himself, "If this man were a prophet, he would know who is touching him and what kind of woman she is—that she is a sinner." . . .

Then [Jesus] turned toward the woman and said to Simon, "Do you see this woman? I came into your house. You did not give me any water for my feet, but she wet my feet with her tears and wiped them with her hair. You did not give me a kiss, but this woman, from the time I entered, has not stopped kissing my feet. You did not put oil on my head, but she has poured perfume on my feet. Therefore, I tell you, her many sins have been forgiven—as her great love has shown. But whoever has been forgiven little loves little."[2]

Tension in the room? One hundred percent! An encounter for the ages that we are still studying. It was certainly different. It was definitely appreciated. The power of the moment gave birth to a breakthrough. Breakthrough for the woman. A big lesson for the disciples. A big miss for the religious. But most importantly, it was *visible for all to see.*

She *stood out.*

Deep Darkness, Shining Lights

Jesus said:

You're here to be light, bringing out the God-colors in the world. God is not a secret to be kept. We're going public with this, as public as a city on a hill. If I make you light-bearers, you don't think I'm going to hide you under a bucket, do you? I'm putting you on a light stand. Now that I've put you there on a hilltop, on a light stand—shine! Keep open house; be generous with your lives. By opening up to others, you'll prompt people to open up with God, this generous Father in heaven.[3]

Contrast. It's when something is strikingly different or stands apart from something else after they're placed side by side. Contrast provides a great context for sensing and appreciating someone or something.

- Two close friends who are polar opposites—perhaps a complete introvert versus total extrovert
- Two different customer experiences when shopping in one store versus the other—one bad and the other awesome
- Seeing large, brilliant, dazzling, multifaceted diamonds displayed across a thick carpet of jet-black velvet—blackness contrasting with brilliance (whoa)
- A giant shooting star rocketing across the dark night sky
- A jet-black tuxedo and bow tie laying over a bright-white tab-collar shirt

Contrasts. Outgoing people help you see and appreciate quieter people. Bad service builds appreciation and activates recognition of good service. Against the black velvet you can see all the brilliance, cuts, clarity, and facets of a diamond. During the daylight hours, you never see a dying star; the night sky is the only way to witness that spectacle. And that tuxedo "pops" so powerfully because black and white so sharply define and contrast with one another.

Low contrast, low appreciation. Higher contrast, higher appreciation.

If salt influences by contact, then light influences *by contrast*. God's people are *intentionally* juxtaposed with spiritual, cultural, and circumstantial darkness in this life. Jesus declared himself "the light of the world,"[4] and in this world, we sense his stark differences and witness his shine *because* he is from heaven—a place of pure light. It's a pattern of God and how he chooses to reveal himself—by contrast—to man. His light against this present darkness.

The people who walk in darkness will see a great light.
For those who live in a land of deep darkness, a light will shine. . . .

For a child is born to us, a son is given to us. The government will rest on his shoulders. And he will be called: Wonderful Counselor, Mighty God, Everlasting Father, Prince of Peace.[5]

This is the crisis we're in: God-light streamed into the world, but men and women everywhere ran for the darkness. They went for the darkness because they were not really interested in pleasing God. Everyone who makes a practice of doing evil, addicted to denial and illusion, hates God-light and won't come near it, fearing a painful exposure. But anyone working and living in truth and reality welcomes God-light so the work can be seen for the God-work it is.[6]

I have come into the world as a light, so that no one who believes in me should stay in darkness.[7]

Jesus—the light—invites. He doesn't make the choice for others; he makes the choice *clear.*

You are light by contrast, living in a world filled with darkness of all kinds, in all dimensions of life, and in all locations of life. You don't and can't make choices for others, but you can—by the way you believe and behave—make the choice of knowing God clearer and more inviting. Your light overflows through the Holy Spirit. In this hour and global moment, God is commanding light to shine, and the Holy Spirit is declaring over all sons of the King . . .

You're here to be light, bringing out the God-colors in the world (Matthew 5:14-16).
Key word? *Here.* Planet Earth. You are on planet Earth for the purpose of "bringing out" God for people to see. In contrast to man's

true colors, the culture's godless colors, and the darker colors of sin and selfishness, people see the colors of the Holy Spirit in you. The Holy Spirit brings out a new integrity in you. You now live undivided between what you believe and how you live and think. Your walk matches your talk, your words are consistent with your ways, and your beliefs and behaviors are aligned. You get a Holy Spirit spine—a confident liberty to think and act differently. Your energy is under the control of the Holy Spirit, and you are clearly focused and disciplined—your eternal destiny is in view. Gone is the fear of men, how they might respond or what they might do. Powerfully present, however, is a holy fear of God and gratitude for what he has done!

Jesus strongly declares that an invisible or hidden Christian is an oxymoron by virtue of that person's identity in him. He wants you visible, end of story. Like Christ, your life is God's light.

In him was life, and that life was the light of all mankind.[8]

You're sons of Light, daughters of Day. We live under wide open skies and know where we stand. So let's not sleepwalk through life like those others. Let's keep our eyes open and be smart. People sleep at night and get drunk at night. But not us! Since we're creatures of Day, let's act like it. Walk out into the daylight sober, dressed up in faith, love, and the hope of salvation.[9]

God says we are destined to live out our *self-perception*. This is why Jesus took great pains to tell us exactly who we are, why we are here, and what our purpose is. The only question is: Whose *perception of you* will prevail and whose voice will you believe?

The Holy Spirit says, "Your life is *my* light."

I'm putting you on a light stand (Matthew 5:14-16).

When Jesus spoke these words, every person immediately understood the context—the inky nighttime darkness of the ancient world. Many of us only know a world that is constantly illuminated, with lights in every room, on phones, in cars, on porches, and in closets. Lights are everywhere. In Jesus' time, people might struggle to see their hands in front of their faces outside and inside the house at night. Large rooms, natural or man-made, offered no light of their own. Our only point of comparison is perhaps during a power outage, when outside and inside illumination are killed. What the average household did have was an oil lamp. So as houses grew dark after sunset, these lamps would be lit, and then the lamps would be put on a special lampstand in an optimal spot to *maximize the light* in the room.

Jesus chose this picture and illustration carefully. His point: God has called you to be light, and to make the best use of you, he has decided your optimal spot on planet Earth, your precise city, street, and building. He doesn't mess around in this way. Place matters. Canaan was not a coincidental neighborhood; it was a promised land. Babylon was not merely a place where Israel was held captive for a while; the Israelites were instructed by Jeremiah during their captivity to seek its peace and prosperity. So what about you? Does your "place" matter to God? Has he somehow misplaced you? You might be tempted to think that, but he is supremely confident in where you are at this very moment. You may not feel that, but he feels nothing but certainty and determination of purpose.

He has placed you strategically in the professional, personal, familial, and social networks you occupy. He has assigned you an area to provide with maximum light in this spiritually dark habitat known as earth where every soul is precious but many are stumbling in the dark. The guy next to you in the gym? Yes. The barista you see every morning? Yes. The neighbor who throws the late-night parties? Yes. Your boss and team at work? Definitely. All are loaded with Kingdom purpose for you. Do you believe that? It might not feel optimal, but if there are people where you are, that's where his "light and lamp" are supposed to be. Your physical locations matter to him—a lot. You are where you are at any given moment because God has determined for you to be there.

> From one man he made all the nations, that they should inhabit the whole earth; and he marked out their appointed times in history and the boundaries of their lands. God did this so that they would seek him and perhaps reach out for him and find him, though he is not far from any one of us.[10]

> And don't be wishing you were someplace else or with someone else. Where you are right now is God's place for you. Live and obey and love and believe right there.[11]

Did you catch that? *Appointed times and boundaries of lands?* God has you where he wants you for now—even if it doesn't feel that way. Your place and his purpose are one as far as he's concerned, but accepting your place as coming from God is essential for finding your purpose. Joseph had to accept prison. Daniel had to accept Babylon. David had to accept the wilderness. Jonah had to swallow Nineveh. Paul was chained to a Roman guard. None of these were optimal from a human point of view, but they were God-appointed. You are a lamp that has been placed by God in your unique and optimal spot to benefit the maximum number of people in that space—the people *assigned* to your spot intentionally. Is that how you see it?

The Holy Spirit says, "I put you there. Your place matters eternally."

"Shine!" Jesus knew the reaction he would get when he said you

don't put a basket over a lamp on its lampstand. His hearers probably thought, *No, you don't!* Or perhaps, *That would be foolish. Who would do that?* Given the level of darkness, a basket move like that would be *unthinkable.* Cities at the tops of hills and lamps sitting strategically atop their lampstands are meant to be easily seen. Light, strategically placed in an optimal spot, is purposed, above all, to shine forth in the darkness in which it is placed. People near it see and sense a form of energy going out and going forth. Whether people see the luminescent glow emitted by an oiled wick set aflame or a sparkling chandelier in a ballroom twinkling above a dance floor, they are seeing an output of energy. Jesus' command to shine is a command to direct your God-given energy outward into your world in God-honoring ways.

> Be energetic in your life of salvation, reverent and
> sensitive before God. That energy is *God's* energy, an
> energy deep within you, God himself willing and working
> at what will give him the most pleasure.
>   Do everything readily and cheerfully—no bickering,
> no second-guessing allowed! Go out into the world
> uncorrupted, a breath of fresh air in this squalid and
> polluted society. Provide people with a glimpse of good
> living and of the living God. Carry the light-giving
> Message into the night so I'll have good cause to be proud
> of you on the day that Christ returns.[12]

Every man has priorities that drive and shape his outbound energy. When people see you, where you are putting your energy, and who's controlling your energy, what do you think they notice? Your energy makes visible what is most important to you—whether your own gods or the one true God.

For most of us, energy is intimately linked to our priorities. Think about the connection between your priorities and your disciplines—the energy you are directing toward a specific purpose. If there's someone you want to date, you'll discipline yourself to be where that person is, learn her relationship status, and at some point, communicate with her in person. If getting a paycheck is important, you'll discipline yourself to get up, shower, eat, and go to work so you can get paid. If getting healthy is important, you'll bring discipline to your eating habits and build in times during the week to get in shape physically. When people see your strong discipline, they see your strong hopes. The prize of God's pleasure is worth the price you are willing to pay. Others see that energy through your disciplined choices.

> No one serving as a soldier gets entangled in civilian affairs, but rather tries to please his commanding officer. Similarly, anyone who competes as an athlete does not receive the victor's crown except by competing according to the rules. The hardworking farmer should be the first to receive a share of the crops.[13]

Shining is putting energy toward your strongest hope, whatever it takes. What's inside us starts overflowing outside us.

> A tree is identified by its fruit. If a tree is good, its fruit will be good. If a tree is bad, its fruit will be bad. You brood of snakes! How could evil men like you speak what is good and right? For whatever is in your heart determines what you say. A good person produces good things from the treasury of a good heart, and an evil person produces evil things from the treasury of an evil heart.[14]

So much darkness all around us. It is thick. It is depressing. Cover up your light now? Hide it? Hit the dimmer switch?

The Holy Spirit says, "No, you don't."

NOTE: An idea section called "Truly Different, Truly Good" is located at the end of the book and highlights some specific ideas for how we can give the Holy Spirit more capacity to "shine" through us.

You'll prompt people to open up with God (Matthew 5:14-16). My soul has prompted me a lot these days—more like yelled at me. Maybe yours has too. Mine is trying to tell me that it is dying to have more than what I have been giving it. Screen flip after screen flip after screen flip, page after page after page, image after image after image, social media post after post. While all this screen time is increasing, soul health is decreasing. Our souls are looking for meaning, but the digital desert we find ourselves wandering in for hours produces only mirages that tease, leaving us unsatisfied and, before bed, unable to find sleep!

We know the reason why, too. It's because human beings require other human beings to see and respond to them and act reciprocally to feel worth, calm our fears, and experience the divine spark of God we were created to know intimately. It's because we are all image-bearers of our Maker, seeking some reflection of him, some feeling of him, some encounter with him consciously and subconsciously every day. It's because we were created to know him in our hearts, souls, and minds. It's because we have made the tool of tech a well of meaning. A line has been crossed.

We have made a good thing the ultimate thing.

For my people have done two evil things: They have abandoned me—the fountain of living water. And they have dug for themselves cracked cisterns that can hold no water at all![15]

People's souls, which are made for God, are getting ripped off by the billions as others make billions in the process. Counterfeits. Imitators. Profit takers. Social manipulators. They prompt us. We bite. They show up again. We bite again. We eat what they're selling, but we are always hungry for more, and the more we eat, the less our souls get basic God nourishment. Oddly, it even feels like something helpful might be happening, which prolongs the digital attachment. Our world has never been more connected, and yet we are, at the same time, less at peace, more anxious, and more at odds with each other than we have ever been. How is God positioned to address this crisis of soul and worldwide opportunity for soul care?

> I'm putting you on a light stand. Now that I've put you there on a hilltop, on a light stand—shine! Keep open house; be generous with your lives. By opening up to others, you'll prompt people to open up with God, this generous Father in heaven.[16]

There is a world full of people walking in darkness who need to encounter the marvelous light of the Holy Spirit overflowing out of you and have their soul collide with his presence. They will see the contrast in you.

The Holy Spirit says: "The world is dying for me, so I am sending it you."

Killing the Lights

Ever been talking to someone and gotten distracted by something going on with his or her face? Could be a smudge of food that they don't know is gracing their mouth or a piece of dried nasal mucus that has moved into plain sight. You are locked on, but they keep on talking. You are not hearing a word, and the errant bit is dominating the encounter to the point of stopping all communication—or at least the receiving part for you. The situation becomes even more tense and difficult when they are talking about something serious, which makes it difficult to interrupt, wipe, blow, snag, and continue interacting. The juxtaposition of "serious" with a booger also makes it difficult to keep a straight face. In the end, we can only enjoy or endure this distracted non-communication for a short time because we love the person too much to keep pretending all is quiet on the facial front. The tension must be broken. The truth must be told. The distraction must be eliminated.

Such is *my life*.

While writing this book, I did my usual post-worship walk to the Welcome Center on our church's patio, where I could chat it up with first-time guests and people in our community. As I took my position, a woman and her husband came up to talk to me. They were super friendly and complimentary, and we got to talking about a new business they were launching in the middle of the COVID pandemic and a building they had signed a lease for. A couple of minutes into the discussion, I was interrupted mid-sentence by the wife, who proceeded to take a Kleenex out of her purse, step forward, pinch my nose, and eliminate an unwelcome piece of dried nasal mucus turtling out of my left nostril.

"There. Got it," she said.

I could have pushed her hand away reflexively as it was on the way in. I could have taken a step back and said, "What are you doing?" I could have reacted post-booger removal and said, "Don't ever do that again" or "I could have gotten that if you told me." I could have overreacted in embarrassment and made more of it than it really was, likely stopping an important conversation. Shocked but not unaware of what had just happened, I said, "Now that's love! Thank you!" We all chuckled and kept on talking. Our conversation and connection continued. The bottom line is that we both wanted the conversation to *continue*, and our actions supported that desire. But *something* had to be done. That booger was killing our conversation, and I had no idea! So she addressed it, and I said thank you.

Boogers kill conversations. Impurities kill salt. Secret sin kills the light.

> Your eye is like a lamp that provides light for your body. When your eye is healthy, your whole body is filled with light. But when it is unhealthy, your body is filled with darkness. Make sure that the light you think you have is not actually darkness. If you are filled with light, with no dark corners, then your whole life will be radiant, as though a floodlight were filling you with light.[17]

Oil lamps have a place on their bottom section that allows the person using them to pour in the oil that the wick draws from to sustain a flame. Jesus, speaking to believers, tells us that our physical bodies are like lamps (containers of the Holy Spirit) that shine light. Just like the lamp must have burnable oil poured into it to act as fuel for the flame, Jesus identifies the process of how we are filled up so that our flames can burn brightly for him. That process starts with our eyes, as we rely on them to take in our environment, take in stimuli, and take in information to process cognitively. This received information (data, imagery, or ideas) is then translated and processed practically, experientially, and behaviorally by the mind, heart, and will.

We do something with it.

We may dismiss it as unimportant. We may store it away for later. We may dwell on it. We may act on it. Every waking minute of every day of our lives, we are "taking in" encounters, environments, ideas, input, experiences, and opportunities, and then processing them toward some decision. It is a miracle of God how it all works. But forces of darkness can also mess with that process in a subtle and sinister way,[18] temporarily extinguishing our lights and their ability to draw people to God.

Otherwise, why say, "Make sure that the light you think you have is not actually darkness"[19]?

It's called spiritual compartmentalization.

But thank God, Jesus warns us against sabotaging our overflow of Holy Spirit power. He goes on to propose being "filled with light"—the opposite condition. He emphasizes the conditional so that the encouragement is also a warning and the warning an encouragement.

> If you are filled with light, with no dark corners, then
> your whole life will be radiant, as though a floodlight
> were filling you with light.[20]

God knows we are susceptible to sin on a daily basis and that, more often than we like, we surrender to FOMO (fear of missing out) and act on an unhealthy thought, temporarily quenching the power of the Holy Spirit's activity in us—and with it, our light's impact in a dark world. That is why he has created a way to restore power quickly and effectively through confession and repentance. It is tried and true, a clear command in God's Word, and a spiritual discipline for saved sinners. It's a Holy Spirit process for getting the power restored—and one that I have needed desperately after blowing it or simply realizing I had been deceived and living a self-ruled life, creating a "dark corner." This word is strong medicine, but it also heals and restores power when obeyed. Lean in—you may not need it now, but you most certainly will need this in your future. Every person who is a light of God needs to know how to restore power and experience relief.

> This, in essence, is the message we heard from Christ and are passing on to you: God is light, pure light; there's not a trace of darkness in him.
>
> If we claim that we experience a shared life with him and continue to stumble around in the dark, we're obviously lying through our teeth—we're not *living* what we claim. But if we walk in the light, God himself being the light, we also experience a shared life with one another, as the sacrificed blood of Jesus, God's Son, purges all our sin.
>
> If we claim that we're free of sin, we're only fooling ourselves. A claim like that is errant nonsense. On the other hand, if we admit our sins—simply come clean about them—he won't let us down; he'll be true to himself. He'll forgive our sins and purge us of all wrongdoing. If we claim that we've never sinned, we out-and-out contradict God—make a liar out of him. A claim like that only shows off our ignorance of God.[21]

Step by step, let's review. Expose the dark corner to the light. You are safe with Jesus. Admit your wrongs. Come clean. Breathe out (confess) to God your sin and the error in your thinking about him and about your sin. Breathe in forgiveness through Christ's person and work for you, which is animated by the power of the Holy Spirit.

Here is a prayer you can use to eliminate a dark corner and restore the power of the Holy Spirit. Pray it now if it applies.

Holy Spirit,

*I need to restore my connection with you. My thinking
has been wrong. I acknowledge I have sinned against you by
directing my own life and allowing a dark corner to remain in my
life against the clear counsel of your character and your Word.
[Name and renounce whatever your dark corner is specifically.]
I know that your light does not blend with darkness. Holy cannot
empower unholy. I thank you that you have forgiven my sins
through Christ's death on the cross for me. I now invite Christ to
again take his place on the throne of my life. Fill me, Holy Spirit,
as you promised in your Word that you would do if I asked in
faith. I pray this in the name of Jesus. I thank you, Holy Spirit, for
directing my life and filling me with light. Thank you for giving
me my identity as your light and for placing me back on my
lampstand for others to see. I pray all this in Jesus' name. Amen.*

3

AROMA THAT SPREADS

I Am Life-Giving

IT WAS CALLED *BEAUTIFUL*, and a bottle of it sat on my desk in my bedroom.

The first time I caught a whiff of it on my girlfriend (now my wife), it was as if a magical spell had been cast over me. *Whoa! That smells wonderful. She smells wonderful. She is wonderful.* True, true, and triple-dog true. So mysteriously powerful was *Beautiful* that when I moved to Texas and we had to date long-distance, all I had to do was grab that bottle off my desk, spray a little on my pillow, lie down, and—*abracadabra!*—I would be transported to different places and times when we were together. My mood would change, and my excitement for a future with Chrissy would go through the roof. I had to be careful about how often I did that, because my phone bill would reflect four-hour conversations on those nights!

A powerful fragrance leaves an impression that marks a special memory or association of that smell to a person *permanently* in the brain. And this power of association is not limited to romance. Here are other powerful scents in my life and where they transport me.

- The smell of *freshly cut grass*. This always takes me back to sunshine-filled days growing up in northern California, playing football and baseball with my buddies, and daydreaming about my future.

- The smell of *gasoline*. This makes me think of the gas station around the corner from my house, where my mom and I would always stop to fill up our station wagon on the way to Moffett Naval Air Base. It also conjures positive memories of all the lawn mowing I did at my house and riding with my brothers on their Harley-Davidson motorcycles. I would sit on the gas tank!

- The smell of *lumpia* frying on the stove. Lumpia is a long, egg roll–type food unique to my culture that is filled with ground beef, ground pork, bamboo shoots, carrots, and cabbage. That smell activates feelings toward my mom, revives memories of luaus at Uncle Eddie's, and makes my mouth water. I re-create that smell in my own house and fry *lumpia* up for my family too!

- The smell of *hospitals*. Not a fan of this one, as I have been called into the presence of death many times during my life.

Our sense of smell is mysterious like that. It can take us places for better or, sadly, for worse. A God-engineered phenomenon? Absolutely.

Molecules. Olfactory nerve. Limbic system.

Tiny molecules enter the nose or mouth and stimulate odor receptors, which send signals up the olfactory nerve straight into your brain's limbic system, translating the information into emotions, feelings, memories, and arousal. Get this: no sense functions more quickly or has a more powerful effect on us than the sense of smell. The science of smell corroborates what we already know intuitively and experientially: *fragrances have an intense power of association.* Inhale a strong scent (good or bad), and the brain starts reacting, mood starts changing, neurons start firing, humans start responding.[1]

Think about it. Cautiously or optimistically, have you ever said to someone, "Do you smell that?"

You can smell real delight and real danger in front of you.

God says that's what happens when *you* are in front of people.

Catching a Whiff of You

Everywhere we go, people breathe in the exquisite fragrance. Because of Christ, we give off a sweet scent rising to God, which is recognized by those on the way of salvation—an aroma redolent with life. But those on the way to destruction treat us more like the stench from a rotting corpse.

2 CORINTHIANS 2:14-16

Just as people cannot remain neutral in the presence of a delightful or dreadful smell, people *cannot not* react to you. We throw off the smell of victory because we are connected to, indwelled by, and controlled by the Spirit of Christ. His presence working in and through us brings satisfaction to God, but it also has the power to bring delight or dread to the people around us. People breathe us into their own spirits, get a sense of who we are, and react to it. We are an aroma that is "redolent," or full of a specific fragrance. In this case, life itself. We are called by God to be a life-giving aroma to the people we meet.

Life-giving versus what? you may be asking. Life-sucking.

Ask yourself: Have you ever been around life-sucking people? They are redolent too—full of a specific fragrance. On one end of the spectrum, some people overflow cynicism and self-loathing; on the opposite end, they overflow narcissism, insecurity, and self-importance. After being with them for any significant length of time, it feels like you've lost a year of your life. You feel very tired and want to avoid them in the future—with good reason.

Jesus is the specific fragrance of God's life—the scent of Jesus rises to God and out toward people. He is life-giving, and his smell is unforgettable in the most positive, Holy Spirit–infused way. He lives in you. More importantly, he gives life to others through you.

That "sweet scent" rises up to God and overflows out of you to people.

God smells your commitment and dedication to him.

Because of Christ, we give off a sweet scent rising to God.
2 CORINTHIANS 2:15

When you live uniquely for God as your audience, your choices change. God senses and enjoys this Holy Spirit discipline much the same way an earthly father enjoys a son imitating his best virtues or not compromising family values under pressure. These spiritual choices for God are the "oils" that supernaturally combine to form a Christ-infused fragrance that rises to God and fills his person with satisfaction and delight. What a thought. God senses delight and "takes in" your choices for him like a pleasing scent!

Think about that the next time you do anything that shows love for him and other people—it's a sweet scent!

But since our conversation is focused on setting the Holy Spirit loose in your world, we need to focus on how Christ's "sweet scent" overflows into the lives of the people God has purposed for you to influence.

People smell Christ's leadership in your life.

In the Messiah, in Christ, God leads us from place to place in one perpetual victory parade.
2 CORINTHIANS 2:14

Supreme military leaders who achieved great victory in the Roman world of the New Testament could receive a designation known as the *vir triumphalis*—the "man of triumph."[2] As the name implies, this man conquered other armies and nations. Upon his return to Rome, a massive parade would be held. This victory parade was so extravagant and over-the-top because his victory was so complete and the scale so large that it merited it. The sights, sounds, and smells all declared a triumph not just for the general but also for his victorious army by association. Picture it:

- Trumpets are sounding off in unison, and large drums are being struck.
- The smell of victory fills the air as incense bearers swing censers, and the sweet aroma fills every space and surrounds every person present.
- A four-horse chariot carries the conquering general. He is dressed in a gold-embroidered purple toga—utterly resplendent in triumph.[3]

- His victorious and vast army marches in column behind their leader as far as the eye can see, sharing the glory of the moment.
- A long train of wagons carries the spoils of his victory—trophies of his triumph.
- The conquered ones—defeated kings and soldiers chained to and being pulled by chariots—accompany the spoils.

Grand, long, sweet-smelling, and spectacular—all to honor the man of triumph and share in his victory. The metaphor is powerful, and God wants you—and all Christ followers—to experience his triumphant leadership in your life—your conquering King leading you to victory after victory after victory after victory! Most notably, God wants culture's leadership and influence over your life to end so that Christ's leadership and influence is *continually* rising, evident in the spaces and places you find yourself.

Every God-born person conquers the world's ways. The conquering power that brings the world to its knees is our faith. The person who wins out over the world's ways is simply the one who believes Jesus is the Son of God.[4]

New leader. New identity. New energy. New and noticeable expression that rises above culture and smells like Christ. Whoever controls your life has power over your "ways" (of thinking and living). People can see and sense when Christ has "taken over" a man's life. They might not be able to put their finger on it at first, but they will be able to tell that you march to the beat of a victorious and different drum. You possess a different set of priorities—eternal ones. You have different way of seeing life and issues—through the lens of God's Word. You have chosen a different way of relating to people, which is less about you and more about others, and some people find this counterintuitive. Your belief in the person, work, and will of Jesus is now informing your behavior.

People smell Christ's character in you.

> Through us, he brings knowledge of Christ. Everywhere
> we go, people breathe in the exquisite fragrance.
> 2 CORINTHIANS 2:14-15

A smell fills air that you—literally—take into yourself. In the same way, when you are in relationship with others and interacting with them for a sufficient length of time, they "take in" your character, expressed in the form of your conduct in their presence. Then they decide if they like the quality!

As Christ fills and forms us inside, the Holy Spirit uses interactions with others to bring his person and presence out in the open for others to sense. Jesus is perfect—the most relationally pleasing man ever to walk planet Earth. He is "exquisite" in ways the Holy Spirit wants reproduced and discerned by others on an increasing basis. When the Bible says of us, "In this world we are like Jesus,"[5] it is speaking of our overflow. For others coming in contact with you, this means everywhere you go:

- You influence without ego.
- You are capable of retaliation but choose reconciliation.
- You pass up power to take up relationship.
- You notice others.
- You are willing to "take the hit" in obedience to God's purpose.
- There is less and less division between what you believe and how you actually live.

- You exchange comfort for discomfort whenever it will show love.
- You deflect flattery and focus on faithfulness.
- You cover and forgive mistakes more than pointing them out.
- You hate for anyone to feel lonely or left out.

These are glimpses of Jesus that people are able to see by knowing you. Everywhere God's man goes, the character of Jesus goes. God's dream for you is that you bear and overflow his likeness.

God knew what he was doing from the very beginning. He decided from the outset to shape the lives of those who love him along the same lines as the life of his Son. The Son stands first in the line of humanity he restored. We see the original and intended shape of our lives there in him.[6]

The Holy Spirit wants to diffuse Christ's character out of you for others to take in.

Fellow followers smell the focus of your life.

We give off a sweet scent rising to God, which is recognized by those on the way of salvation—an aroma redolent with life.

2 CORINTHIANS 2:14-15

Smells linger—they trail a presence. Smells are distinct—they are identified with a source. Smells are judged—there is no such thing as a neutral odor. When someone encounters the Holy Spirit in a Christian, it is just like encountering a smell. God's intention is for our lives to elicit a reaction. More specifically, when we are among believers, our "smell" should be pleasing, life-giving, and encouraging to them.

Knowing and sensing Christ through your attitudes and actions:

- Creates excitement for another believer (or should!) as you are both members of God's victorious army and connected to the joy of his triumph.
- Sets a mood of safety for another believer. You are family.
- Creates anticipation in other believers to hear about your personal faith journey.
- Invites common purposes into the discussion.
- Offers opportunities in the area of encouragement.
- Provides healthy accountability directly and indirectly to God.
- Links your spirits of gratitude and love for what Jesus has done for you.
- Unites your eternal futures and experiences.

Aromas in a triumphal procession were pleasing and *life-giving* to the victorious. The smell of Jesus in another believer is intended by God to have the same effect. When the man of God is with the people of God, he reminds his fellow believers of the sweetness of Christ's victory. We are one in victory, we are one in experience, and we have one heart for our conquering Commander.

So speak encouraging words to one another. Build up hope so you'll all be together in this, no one left out, no one left behind. I know you're already doing this; just keep on doing it.[7]

Nonbelievers—by choice—smell what they don't desire.

> But those on the way to destruction treat us more like the
> stench from a rotting corpse.
> **2 CORINTHIANS 2:16**

While others who believe and have received the gospel react positively to you, those who have that same knowledge of Jesus but reject him are condemned by it and do not like being reminded of that reality. What smells sweet to an actively professing believer smells like decaying meat in hot weather to an actively rejecting nonbeliever. You are a stench. Your "smell"—which nonbelievers associate with Jesus—lingers. That means the Holy Spirit at work in you and overflowing out of you is colliding with another spirit flowing out of nonbelievers. Just as we cannot be neutral about a smell, those who are nonbelievers by choice cannot encounter the aroma of Christ in you without reacting to you negatively. The spirit in them won't allow it now that you are on the winning side. Jesus was clear: what they did to him they will do to you once they get a whiff of him in you. Specifically, they will reject you, actively avoid you, or even persecute you when they sense the smell of victory you possess in Christ.

In a world where everyone wants to be liked and have followers, the brutal reality is that more people will reject Jesus than accept him. That intentional decision on their part amplifies the interaction and reaction they have with others who have chosen differently. In other words, your choice and your victory mean their choice and utter defeat are highlighted in much the same way the parade of triumph did for the defeated captives. Humiliation does not feel good, and the sadness within gives birth to an anger that flows out and toward any person they connect to their unhappy ending. That sadness is also exploited and used by the evil one to control their actions.

Once you were dead because of your disobedience and your many sins. You used to live in sin, just like the rest of the world, obeying the devil—the commander of the powers in the unseen world. He is the spirit at work in the hearts of those who refuse to obey God.[8]

They make themselves offensive to God and everyone else by trying to keep us from telling people who've never heard of our God how to be saved. They've made a career of opposing God, and have gotten mighty good at it. But God is fed up, ready to put an end to it.[9]

When you give off the smell of victory, you ignite the spirit of the defeated. Jesus said this comingling of good and evil side by side would mark our time on earth and that it is something God allows. As the "aroma of Christ to the perishing," we must accept negative reactions until his eternal victory is sealed and evil opposition is eternally consumed by the fire of his power.

The Kingdom of Heaven is like a farmer who planted good seed in his field. But that night as the workers slept, his enemy came and planted weeds among the wheat, then slipped away. When the crop began to grow and produce grain, the weeds also grew.

The farmer's workers went to him and said, "Sir, the field where you planted that good seed is full of weeds! Where did they come from?"

"An enemy has done this!" the farmer exclaimed.

"Should we pull out the weeds?" they asked.

"No," he replied, "you'll uproot the wheat if you do. **Let both grow together until the harvest.** Then I will tell the harvesters to sort out the weeds, tie them into bundles, and burn them, and to put the wheat in the barn."[10]

God's Kingdom is advancing toward an ultimate victory, or harvest. God's Kingdom is also at war and is being opposed until that moment. While God is willing that all should escape judgment, he knows the majority of people will choose it.

The Holy Spirit says your smell of victory will energize the soldiers of defeat.

People smell humility.

> We stand in Christ's presence when we speak; God looks us in the face. We get what we say straight from God and say it as honestly as we can.
> **2 CORINTHIANS 2:17**

Like Paul, every believer should be dumbfounded that God would use them to advance his purposes based on who he is and who we are—a huge gap at every level! And it is that gap between us and God that cultivates and animates Holy Spirit–given humility in us and through us. In fact, when accurately understood, it should be the most humbling force in our lives and shape our actions and interactions. Proper humility (as opposed to false) is simple and powerful when recognized by others—easy to see and sense. Think about it.

- Someone is present who is more knowledgeable or skilled than you in some pursuit or category. You recognize that. Then you humbly defer to them in the matter. Why? They are wiser and better. Humility.

- Credit or attention is given to you alone for a success or achievement. You credit the people around you who helped make it possible. Why? The reality called for it. Humility.

- A boss or mentor focuses on elevating and advancing you at work more than they look out for their own upward mobility. Why? They know and see the reality that long-term success (versus short-term personal gain) calls for it. Humility.

In the same way, God, God's Word, and God's presence are realities that call for humility to win the moment and overflow.

Humility is having a proper view of yourself in the presence of others, but accomplishing this in a digital culture dedicated to social self-celebration is a battle. On one side, you have natural insecurity and pride common to all human beings; on the other side, you have humility and confidence rooted in God's acceptance. One inner reality allows for proper humility, and you put others above yourself. The other is a hot mess of selfishness. Sadly, one continuous, never-ending run of other-centered humility isn't possible. But the good news is that a follower of Jesus has the Holy Spirit dwelling within.

The first way the Holy Spirit brings to life Christ's humility is by reproducing his character.

> Come to me, all of you who are weary and carry heavy
> burdens, and I will give you rest. Take my yoke upon you.
> Let me teach you, because I am humble and gentle at
> heart, and you will find rest for your souls. For my yoke is
> easy to bear, and the burden I give you is light.[11]

Jesus is humble and people feel less burdened in his presence. The Holy Spirit reproduces this quality in Jesus' followers, and in their presence, others feel lighter versus heavier, encouraged versus discouraged, and helped versus used. When you overflow Christ's humility, others supernaturally smell *him* and are attracted to him in you! It's palpable.

The second way the Holy Spirit brings about Christ's humility is by reminding you:

- He is the Creator; you were created.
- He is the Vine; you are the branch.
- He is the Potter; you are the clay.
- He is the Shepherd; you are a sheep.
- He is the Savior; you are the one who was rescued.
- He is the treasure; you are a common jar that holds it.
- He is the Master; you are the servant.
- He is immortal; you are mortal.
- He is the fragrance; you are the vessel from which it *overflows*.

God knows who he is. The Holy Spirit reminds us who we are. When we know who we are in relation to who God is, then we stop acting like or trying to be God. God is always in the *A* position, and we are always in the *B* position. He is above; we are below. He is in charge; we submit. He alone is independent and self-sufficient; we are limited and God-dependent. His vision and intention prevail; we are surrendered to them. He is our rescuer; we are the saved ones. He is the wonder, the awe, and the glory to behold; we are simply vessels who reflect God's wonderful qualities into the world.

> He has shown you, O mortal, what is good. And what does the LORD require of you? To act justly and to love mercy and to walk humbly with your God.[12]

The Holy Spirit wants Christ's humility overflowing into your world.

A Sweet Stench?

I was what you might call a liquid hydrogen convert to Christianity.

If you have ever bumped into anyone who has "seen the light," you know what I am talking about—very excited, very passionate, tons of energy, and fully committed at the start. That was me—all jacked up, lit up, *en fuego*. For many, I am sure, the label "whack job" would have fit, or at least WARNING: HIGHLY FLAMMABLE MATERIAL. Some of my friends who witnessed my initial transformation would confirm that. This simply meant I was not ashamed to be called a Christian, spread the aroma of Christ, and champion my victorious Savior. It also meant that I liberally wielded the sword of the Spirit—the Bible.

I was *thrilled* to be going to heaven. I was *relieved* that my sins were forgiven. I was *hopeful* about my purpose for the first time in my life. God gave me new and positive *identities*—I am salt, I am light, I am an aroma of life. That's a big momentum shift for a guy whose classmates voted him "the life of the party" and whom neighborhood parents told their kids to avoid. With one life-altering decision, a major explosion of passion and purpose had erupted within me, exploding ten kilotons' worth of spiritual fuel. That's the upside of my Holy Spirit slingshot.

The other highly volatile mixture of accelerant residing inside of me was the stuff I was hoping my newfound faith would magically erase. These unstable elements of my character included patterns of thinking, mixed motives, emotional injuries in need of healing, hidden insecurities, longings, disappointments, shame, discontentment, and a deeply rooted need for acceptance. The Holy Spirit wanted to work those out in his own way over time.

What I didn't know was that Satan wanted to exploit them in his own way over time.

Jesus' words to his disciples that we discussed earlier tell the whole story: "Make sure that the light you think you have is not actually darkness."[13] Just like salt can be rendered useless and light's power can be cut off, your aroma (Christ in you) can distance others from God rather than attract them. In a reframing of Jesus' words about light, I hear the Holy Spirit issuing this caution to all followers of Christ: "Make sure the sweet smell you think you're spreading is not actually a stench."

If the devil couldn't take away my salvation and connection to Jesus, he would do his best to make that connection as unhealthy and toxic as possible. His aim was simple: take an authentic conversion and attempt to make it shallow, synthetic, and full of contradictions. How, you say? He used the residual emotional and mental character issues left inside of me to fashion a faith around the broken parts of my manhood—the parts that make anything they touch self-centered, dysfunctional, and willing to entertain sin.

Satan probably has a similar strategy with other believers. I can just see Satan telling his emissaries:

- **Get him focused on certain behaviors and performance markers.** He'll over-perform because he's a pleaser and a competitor.

- **Foster self-righteousness.** He'll take the credit for his own goodness instead of crediting the work of the Cross and giving God the glory. Spiritual pride is as good as any form of pride.

- **Cause him to worry** about things he shouldn't worry about, like maintaining his image as the perfect Christian. Take the focus off the internal (character change) and put it on the external (behaviors).

- **Create a public-private split.** Make him one person publicly and another person privately who secretly struggles with things his religious image will never allow him to talk about.

- **Create a false sense of security and dependence on his behaviors *for God* versus finding his security *in God*.** When he messes up, he'll feel guilty and convince himself he'll never measure up. You know how many we've seen throw in the towel.

- **Make him hide his true self** with other Christians—the ones who struggle with flaws and temptations. The longer he hides his true self, the higher the wall will become, making it impossible for him to reveal who he really is. He'll be miserable, feel stuck, and want to go back to old habits of coping with stress and pressure.

- **Use his religious image to make him appear narrow-minded, ignorant, and superstitious,** blind to reality and the real need people have for compassion, mercy, and love. Use his faith expression to alienate rather than connect.

- **Encourage him to think negatively toward or be suspicious of "normal" people so he can feel better about himself.** He will replace God's power of judgment with his own, further separating him from people he could lead to Christ.

- **Use his faith to cultivate a false sense of control,** authority, and power that is self-serving.

- **Motivate him through fear and guilt.** Breed spiritual insecurities and doubts. Magnify spiritual failures.

- **Create distance between him and non-Christians** by making him think they will lead him astray. Give him a holy huddle to keep him all warm and fuzzy. He will isolate himself from people who could benefit from his presence.

Those are the tactics evil will engage in to turn you from a pleasing scent to a "sweet" stench. If successful, what you will see is more harm being done than good. Evil loves dysfunctional spirituality.

Jesus confronted it, because it smells horrible *in his name*.

Woe to you, teachers of the law and Pharisees, you hypocrites! You give a tenth of your spices—mint, dill and cumin. But you have neglected the more important matters of the law—justice, mercy and faithfulness. You should have practiced the latter, without neglecting the former. You blind guides! You strain out a gnat but swallow a camel.[14]

Good intentions. Wrong target. God followers have been rope-a-doped by Satan into becoming judgmental nitpickers. The spiritual life is not an accounting class. We forget how to block and tackle spiritually. We need to be reminded of the character of Jesus and overflow more justice, mercy, and faithfulness on others!

Woe to you, teachers of the law and Pharisees, you hypocrites! You clean the outside of the cup and dish, but inside they are full of greed and self-indulgence. Blind Pharisee! First clean the inside of the cup and dish, and then the outside also will be clean.[15]

God followers too easily fall for the oldest trick in the book: *I can fake it*. Conviction without character is a CATASTROPHE. Bad character inside will never produce proper influence outside, just like no rearrangement of spoiled eggs can *ever* produce a good omelet. So start over! Work this puppy from the inside out beginning with the eggs (your motives). Find good ones, and then the omelet you are serving up (your influence) will both smell and taste better to those around you who care to sample it. There's nothing worse than a rotten egg omelet.

> Woe to you, teachers of the law and Pharisees, you hypocrites! You are like whitewashed tombs, which look beautiful on the outside but on the inside are full of the bones of the dead and everything unclean. In the same way, on the outside you appear to people as righteous but on the inside you are full of hypocrisy and wickedness.[16]

Jesus says then and now, "I want spiritual integrity. I want talk *and* walk. I want belief *and* behaviors. I want words *and* ways. I want intentions *and* actions. A pretty tombstone and flowers on the top cannot negate the reality of a decomposing carcass under the surface. *You're acting!* You might bamboozle the public, but God says, 'I see the real you. Have you forgotten how I evaluate my leaders?'"

> The Lord does not look at the things people look at. People look at the outward appearance, but the Lord looks at the heart.[17]

Satan's goal is dysfunctional spirituality—making Christ followers into a sweet stench. He is working overtime to create inauthentic, judgmental, insecure, and insulated Christians who are so in love with *acting* Christian (the outward appearances) that they do not have a clue what it means to *be* Christian. They are uncomfortable around nonbelievers; they don't know how to engage them, and they make "spiritual" excuses for not connecting with them.

- "They drink a lot."
- "He identifies as same-sex attracted."
- "They don't go to church."
- "He's always using foul language."
- "He's Muslim."
- "He's a liberal."
- "He's a conservative."
- "He's been divorced three times."

And so on. It's as if they expect non-Christians to act like Christians! These kinds of religious attitudes confuse our decision-making, slow our willingness to act lovingly toward people, and make our sweet smell a stench.

The Holy Spirit does not want a stench turned loose in our world.

I think that is why Jesus was so emphatic in the parable of the Good Samaritan. Religious guys are the bad example! They are not neighbors. They are too synthetic, shallow, and scared to reach out to people not like themselves. They are a stench to a watching world. They are dysfunctional, presenting as righteous but responding irrationally to the huge needs around them. In the end, it's about *them*, their agendas, and their convenience, while people are dying by the side of the road. They have rules of engagement that say to the outsider: *You can meet me on my terms when it is convenient for me. I refuse to get messy, so let me pass by on the other side of the road.*

Real faith that smells really sweet like Jesus, on the other hand, breaks all the rules of man to meet a need. The authentic aroma of Christ lingers on the same side of the road as the traumatized and forgotten. A genuine faith aroma is more about divesting yourself of your own dignity in order to restore someone else's—like Jesus did coming to earth. Sincere faith means not being at peace until someone else's peace is secured. The Samaritan in the parable, according to Jesus, is the true aroma of Christ, and his actions are the influencing behaviors of a real man of God.

In contrast, men who bark rules from across the road rather than moving toward need with power and grace cause the exquisite aroma of Christ to go stenchy. As U2 front man Bono has said, "People who are spiritually abused can rarely approach the subject of religion with fresh faith. They wince and they twitch."[18]

This is why it's so important for men to stay closely connected to the Holy Spirit. He is helping us become like Jesus, infusing us with the aroma of Christ. Anything that diverts focus from God— even when the goal is to draw people to God—repels people from God, serving the agenda of the devil.

So how do you measure aroma versus stench?

As Jesus explained to the religious guy with whom he shared the parable of the Good Samaritan, we measure how religious we have become by how distant we are from the real needs of those around us who need our help. If our practice of faith in Christ, or our aroma . . .

- projects judgment toward outsiders
- distances us from fellow human beings in need
- makes *us* feel better more than making *others* feel relief and help
- limits our audience exclusively to other Christians
- labels nonbelievers or believers negatively
- creates "second-class" Christians
- emphasizes behaviors that define true believers

. . . then rest assured that Satan is making us stenchy. Jesus says, *"Fight this!"*

The Holy Spirit wants to spread a sweet aroma in your world today.

Use the following prayer to express your desire.

Holy Spirit,

I want to be the aroma of Christ that people experience. Fill me and work in me to make me more and more like Jesus and less and less like the world. Help people notice your leadership in my life as I simply follow your voice, your will, and your way. Help people feel your character as I boldly pursue change and the fruit you produce. Help me intentionally encourage fellow followers of Christ and thereby spread the triumphant joy of the victorious, uniting our purpose and future. Help me share my story and spread the exquisite nature of Christ even among those who reject me, leading some to belief and salvation. In every circle of influence you place me in, never let my faith be about me but about Christ and his victory. Search my motives. Cleanse my heart. Reveal any impurity. Replace it with spiritual integrity. And because I know the evil one desires to pollute my influence, I accept and exercise my authority in you to bind any false spirit of religion and release the aroma of Christ into the world. I ask for more and more life to come from you to me so that I can be life-giving. In Jesus' name I pray. Amen.

PART II

OVERFLOWING ENERGY

4

AVAILABLE TO GOD
IN MY CONTEXT

I Am Releasable for God's Purposes

COACH ALI'S PRACTICES were so good that I spectated with a pen and journal in hand to script them for my son's soccer team, which I was still coaching at the time. Whenever possible, I would come to my daughter's practices to watch and learn from a man who was coaching on a whole new level. Between watching practices and going to games, which usually involved travel, Ali and I ended up talking and instant messaging (the precursor to texting) a lot. Once this dialogue started happening, God started talking to me about Ali and why my spectator role at practices and games had a much larger purpose than soccer. God placed me in this context. This moment was *his* doing.

- I am a dad.
- My daughter is an athlete.
- She is on a specific team with a specific coach.
- Ali came all the way to Southern California from Louisville, Kentucky, and landed with this team.

- I am getting to know my daughter's coach on a more personal level.
- The Holy Spirit is at work.
- The Holy Spirit is in me.
- Ali is not a Christian.
- God loves Ali.
- I have both opportunity and ability to connect with Ali.
- I believe our relationship has been intentionally orchestrated.
- I have a message of hope that can impact Ali's future forever.

Those are just the facts. That is the context. Nothing had happened yet. But as my awareness of God's presence and purpose grows, I start to think, connect the dots, and focus on being mindful, flexible, and adaptable to *whatever role* God wants me to play. It is becoming increasingly clear that I don't have to orchestrate an opportunity at all. God placed me here to overflow into the situations and people already present. All I have to do is make myself *available* to the Holy Spirit in my context.

I was enjoying where all of this was headed until an unexpected instant message from Ali popped onto my laptop screen at work with a *buhloop* sound:

> *Hey, Kenny. It looks like I won't be coaching the team anymore. The director and I don't see eye to eye on some of the camps I did over the summer for him or the compensation I received.*

I was shocked by the news, but the Holy Spirit said to me, "This is the door you have been praying for." Having previously put myself at his disposal, I was ready for this overflow moment. What happened next is nothing short of a miracle. I responded:

Well, Ali, I don't know if you are a praying man, but I
believe we have been placed together for a reason.

After I hit Send, a flood of thoughts crossed my mind, which
included:

- *I am not close enough to him yet.*
- *He is Muslim.*
- *I might have just ended the conversation right there.*
- *He is going to light me up for bringing God into the*
  conversation.

Then I saw little bubbles flashing on my screen indicating
activity, and after the bubbles it read:

. . . Ali is typing.

I prayed and then made two phone calls—one to to Chrissy
and another to friends who knew Ali. I asked them to pray for this
conversation while he typed his instant message for what seemed
to be an extraordinarily long time. *Buhloop!* Ali finally responded:

I have been searching for a conversation with God ever since
I was a young boy. My mother told me never to reject Jesus
because he was a special man. I never forgot this.

You never know what will unfold after a simple encounter in
your context.

That conversation through instant messaging led to Ali believing in the person and work of Christ for himself. That was twenty
years ago, and since that time, Ali has led an incredible life of
impact for Christ in the world of youth and collegiate soccer,

placing himself at the disposal of the Holy Spirit to impact those God brings into his path. Many of his players have introduced themselves to me as the fruit—so to speak—of his ministry, connecting that moment in my life as a spectating father to our divine appointment through instant messenger. From then to now, he has personally impacted thousands upon thousands of youth athletes at camps across the world and is currently directing a large outreach to college athletes. Not surprisingly, he would never highlight anything I just said. He is too focused on what the Holy Spirit is doing daily in the lives of the athletes he serves and how he can play his part.

As Ali and I continue to do ministry together and support each other, our friendship reminds me every day of the importance of being and staying available to what the Holy Spirit is doing in any given situation. It is weighty.

The big wheels of Holy Spirit impact turn on the small axles of our availability.

Whoever, Wherever, Whenever

It starts there. It *always* starts there, doesn't it?

You can know who God says you are and know intellectually the implications of being salt, light, and an aroma of Christ, but experientially it boils down to moments when you put yourself at the disposal of the Holy Spirit to be used for his purposes. Cultivating this lifestyle in practice calls for a specific view of time and space, a willingness to serve a role within it, and faith flexible enough to reach people in a variety of contexts.

Being available to the Holy Spirit means being mindful of eternity in every opportunity. What we see with our physical eyes veils what we can see and sense through the supernatural presence of the Holy Spirit and our connection to him. He puts us in touch with spiritual realities, plans, and forces that are at work in our context, and these revelations are purposed to gain our focus and attention. The fact that powerful Kingdom realities are being played out in the midst of regular life makes this necessary. The Holy Spirit offers to all believers a revelation of the Kingdom realm they belong to. However, our part is to set our hearts and minds on faith in God, adopt his perspective, and track with his active plan in our midst. Our eyes and heart must be "on a swivel," in military terms—constantly alert to supernatural movement so that we don't miss anything. The Holy Spirit cannot be set loose through us in any environment if the Holy Spirit radar system of our hearts and minds is not in the *ON* position.

> So if you're serious about living this new resurrection life with Christ, *act* like it. Pursue the things over which Christ presides. Don't shuffle along, eyes to the ground, absorbed with the things right in front of you. Look up, and be alert to what is going on around Christ—that's where the action is. See things from *his* perspective.[1]

> So we fix our eyes not on what is seen, but on what is unseen, since what is seen is temporary, but what is unseen is eternal.[2]

Scripture encourages us to start with being alert to what God may want to do. A way to do that is simply to pray and ask God for his wisdom and insight prior to being with people. Then start looking at people and the context God has placed you in from a Kingdom perspective—that God is sovereign and has you here for a purpose with this specific group. Next—and it sounds simple—go with the flow! No need to manipulate conversations or situations. You will know when to either pray into something, comment intentionally, or share something from your life. If the

Holy Spirit is leading, you don't have to force anything. Instead, remain fixed and locked in on the eternal.

Your mind focuses on what your eyes track. Try it. They work in tandem. I become alert to something, start tracking it with my eyes, and my mind processes what I see, preparing my body to move, stay put, say something, or plan a course of action for later. Spiritually, this is how the Holy Spirit works with a follower who is mindful or "alert to what is going on around Christ" and seeing things from his perspective. God's Spirit helps a believer to see people and situations the way God sees them and then provides plans for a next step. The emphasis of Scripture is for the believer to actively partner with the Holy Spirit and protect the connection. In doing so, we preserve and advance the "opportunity" God has invited us into for his purposes.

> Be very careful, then, how you live—not as unwise but as wise, making the most of every opportunity, because the days are evil. Therefore do not be foolish, but understand what the Lord's will is. Do not get drunk on wine, which leads to debauchery. Instead, be filled with the Spirit, speaking to one another with psalms, hymns, and songs from the Spirit. Sing and make music from your heart to the Lord, always giving thanks to God the Father for everything, in the name of our Lord Jesus Christ.[3]

The command is, "Be very careful, then, how you live"—a mindset of being alert to Kingdom opportunities God may be presenting to you in your context. Being filled with the Holy Spirit means being controlled by him within that opportunity. What follows is the result when you are filled with the Holy Spirit and listening to him: you will start speaking spiritual words and taking spiritual actions "in the name of our Lord Jesus Christ."

Be mindful. Be filled. Then be bold!

Being available to the Holy Spirit means being flexible in every opportunity. The saying, "He was in the right place at the right time," suggests that an opportunity presented itself to someone without his foreknowledge and only a *minimal effort* of recognition and action was required to trigger a *maximum result.* It is as though the situation were "pre-baked" and a specific opportunity collided with a random person coincidentally. So often in the Bible we read about God arranging situations that—to the man—initially appeared random. But not to God. Far from it. So many of these circumstances are a mosaic of people, time, and location that he intentionally pieces together for a higher purpose. We are not looking down on the situation like God is—we are looking straight at it. We are not seeing God moving people into proximity with one another—we are simply traveling our own road, putting one foot in front of the other, one day at a time. In these instances, the man of God remains flexible and is prepared to adjust quickly. As God is orchestrating, a follower's responsibility is to cooperate in the moment and do whatever the Holy Spirit says to do next.

God orchestrates. The Holy Spirit communicates. We cooperate.

Having become mindful of the supernatural realities occurring around us, now the step of faith is to stay flexible and responsive to the Holy Spirit's prompting *within a circumstance.* Because God sees and knows what we cannot, we need to be ready to move at a moment's notice again and again, if necessary, to get into position for a Kingdom collision. It's about the right man *yielding* to the Holy Spirit's influence to seize the opportunity God has *already prepared* for him.

I looked for someone to stand up for me against all this,
to repair the defenses of the city, to take a stand for me

and stand in the gap to protect this land so I wouldn't have to destroy it. I couldn't find anyone. Not one.[4]

A need. An opportunity. A specific space. A specific place. A "gap" man for God.

There is nothing random about the needs God sees and how he wants to work with you and me. We have a payload of Holy Spirit assets he wants to bring into situations to further his purposes and bring him glory uniquely. Knowing when to use which assets of the Spirit requires thoughtful discernment or sometimes disciplined self-control, depending on what he desires to call out of us in any given moment.

But the fruit of the Spirit is love, joy, peace, forbearance, kindness, goodness, faithfulness, gentleness and self-control. Against such things there is no law. Those who belong to Christ Jesus have crucified the flesh with its passions and desires. Since we live by the Spirit, let us keep in step with the Spirit.[5]

It is these specific qualities expressed in personal action that God seeks to bring into relationships and situations through us. Sometimes this happens in planned, deliberate ways over time, but many times it happens spontaneously in the moment. In those instances, prompt recognition and timely cooperation demand flexibility.

Philip is great example of this flexibility or "keep[ing] in step with the Spirit."[6] In Samaria, he was told by an angel to head toward Jerusalem, then merge onto a desert road that would take him to Gaza, roughly one hundred miles to the south. No explanation, just "Go." He was available and flexible as God's plan unraveled *spontaneously*.

Now an angel of the Lord said to Philip, "Go south to the road—the desert road—that goes down from Jerusalem to Gaza." So he started out, and on his way he met an Ethiopian eunuch, an important official in charge of all the treasury of the Kandake (which means "queen of the Ethiopians"). This man had gone to Jerusalem to worship, and on his way home was sitting in his chariot reading the Book of Isaiah the prophet. The Spirit told Philip, "Go to that chariot and stay near it."

Then Philip ran up to the chariot and heard the man reading Isaiah the prophet. "Do you understand what you are reading?" Philip asked.

"How can I," he said, "unless someone explains it to me?" So he invited Philip to come up and sit with him.

This is the passage of Scripture the eunuch was reading:

> "He was led like a sheep to the slaughter,
>   and as a lamb before its shearer is silent,
>   so he did not open his mouth.
>
> In his humiliation he was deprived of justice.
>   Who can speak of his descendants?
>   For his life was taken from the earth."

The eunuch asked Philip, "Tell me, please, who is the prophet talking about, himself or someone else?" Then Philip began with that very passage of Scripture and told him the good news about Jesus.

As they traveled along the road, they came to some water and the eunuch said, "Look, here is water. What can stand in the way of my being baptized?" And he gave orders to stop the chariot. Then both Philip and the eunuch went down into the water and Philip baptized him.[7]

Philip was called spontaneously into a specific space with a specific person doing a specific thing. It shows his true availability to the Holy Spirit and his flexibility within the opportunity. Follow the unseen script of these events as they unfold in real time with some real thoughts:

"Get on the road to Gaza." That's it. No reason.

He starts walking south.

"On his way . . ." Philip bumps into a highly placed Ethiopian seeker.

Next order: *"Go stand next to his chariot."* He runs to get there.

Catching his breath, he leans in. He listens. He hears the Ethiopian reading.

Mental processing . . . "Can't be! Is he reading Isaiah talking about the Messiah?"

Answer: "Yes! I recognize that passage of Scripture."

Holy Spirit says: *"Now ask him a question."*

Here goes nothing: "Excuse me. Couldn't help but overhear. Do you know . . . ?"

Answer: "No. But who is this being described?"

Mental processing . . . "Hahaha, Holy Spirit! He's sincere. Really? You are amazing."

Holy Spirit says: *"Well, dive in and tell him the answer, Christ follower."*

Philip tells the Ethiopian about Jesus.

The Ethiopian believes that Jesus is the Son of God.

Philip ends up traveling with the Ethiopian in his chariot.

"As they traveled . . ." the Ethiopian sees some water. Here
we go!

Holy Spirit says to the Ethiopian, *"Go and be baptized."*

The Ethiopian asks Philip, "Any problem with me going
public with my new faith?"

Holy Spirit says to Philip: *"Get down. Get wet. Get him fully
identified with Christ."*

Philip is available. God is nimble to need. Philip is mindful and
flexible. The Ethiopian is grateful. Both are wet.

Years later, Philip says, "Did I ever tell you the one about the
Ethiopian I bumped into on the way to Gaza? Yeah, going to Gaza
was never part of the plan!"

*Being available to the Holy Spirit means being adaptable in every
opportunity.* Being adaptable—as a person—means that you are
not rigid, that you can change the way you present yourself to fit
different types of situations. For the man of God, however, being
adaptable does not mean compromising your core identity. It's
having the ability and faith to connect *meaningfully* with people
different from yourself without compromising who you are or
what you believe. Think about it from God's perspective. What use
is it to be available for the Holy Spirit to use but only be "usable"
with one type of person in one type of culture in one kind of way?
Specialists, generalists, artists, metallurgists, militarists, harpists,
adventurists, agriculturalists, activists, you name it—the story of
God's redemptive plan revealed in Scripture reflects every dimension of profession and passion. Add to this all of those fruity assets
of the Holy Spirit mentioned earlier as well as all of the gifts of the
Spirit. God uses a kaleidoscope of gifts and skills. This is exactly
why Jesus offended the rigid and one-dimensional religious men
of his day. He was "stretchy" but strong.

The Son of Man came eating and drinking, and they
say, "Here is a glutton and a drunkard, a friend of tax
collectors and sinners." But wisdom is proved right by her
deeds.[8]

Malleable. Friend of sinners?

Jesus was not the Messiah anyone expected him to be, and his
story would have been the lyrics of a good country song in his day.
He had friends in low places and in high places. He reached Jews.
He reached Romans. He reached hated Samaritans. He connected
with men. He connected with, protected, and defended women.
He was the Messiah for prostitutes, traitors to the nation, lepers,
and the lame. He was the champion of the least, the lost, and the
left out. He was holy, and he was human. He was gracious, and
he was truthful. He was compassionate, and he was convicted. He
could connect with every man, but he would not compromise his
commitment to the Father for any man. His ability to influence
so many people across such a wide variety of classes and races can
be attributed to his adaptability. In Jesus, God's love met people
where they were instead of demanding they stretch to meet him.
This is exactly what he said the Spirit of God would empower
him to do.

> The Spirit of the LORD is upon me, for he has anointed
> me to bring Good News to the poor. He has sent me to
> proclaim that captives will be released, that the blind will
> see, that the oppressed will be set free, and that the time
> of the LORD's favor has come.[9]

When Jesus announced how he would set the Holy Spirit
loose in his world and context, he identified categories of people
who felt far from God but who were being marginalized by those

representing God—women, ethnic minorities, people with physical disabilities, or those who had violated moral norms of the day. Jesus stretched himself to come to earth. He stretched the boundaries of his native culture to reach those who did not belong to it. He stretched his arms out to be nailed to a cross in order to make his love available across cultures, across centuries, and across man's limited self-perceptions, for every human being.

Available. Malleable. Stretching. Intentional. Loving.

This is the spirit of God's available man.

Even though I am free of the demands and expectations of everyone, I have voluntarily become a servant to any and all in order to reach a wide range of people: religious, nonreligious, meticulous moralists, loose-living immoralists, the defeated, the demoralized—whoever. I didn't take on their way of life. I kept my bearings in Christ—but I entered their world and tried to experience things from their point of view. I've become just about every sort of servant there is in my attempts to lead those I meet into a God-saved life. I did all this because of the Message. I didn't just want to talk about it; I wanted to be *in* on it![10]

In other words, as a man who is available and at the disposal of the Holy Spirit, I will do whatever it takes to make a meaningful connection with people without compromising my commitment to Jesus and his commands. This adaptable approach is not pursued in reaction to culture but in full regard of God, his love for people, and his sacrifice for me. This means—like Jesus—you will find me stretching to connect with people not like me and engaging in activities that other believers might condemn as inconsistent with a Christian lifestyle. This means I will offer myself to people who *don't believe* to serve them and treat them as I would want to be treated when I am in need. This means I am going to be generous with my time, prayers, and resources without thought to blood, faith, ethnic, cultural, moral, or political affiliation. Whenever I am challenged by any of these, I simply remember Jesus' model. He broke the rules of religious culture when he needed to connect with people who felt lonely, in the margins, out of the "club," or far from God.

While I was writing this book, a man approached me at the end of a men's session at my church, complaining that a certain word that rhymes with *brass* was used in a testimony by one of our pastors. He went on to tell me that such a word had no place in a gathering among men of God. I could see where he was coming from. It would not be appropriate in most settings. So I asked him if he knew Jesus and was going to heaven, to which he replied, "Yes." I then went on to tell him that the outreach he was attending was not designed to reach saved people who knew Jesus already—although many parts of it would fuel his faith and challenge him to take a step of faith.

I said, "You're in! You are going to heaven. This weekend is specifically designed musically and from the stage to be very meaningful for the demographic we are trying to reach—twenty-five- to fifty-year-old men who do not profess faith in Christ."

I told him to read 1 Corinthians 9:19-23 (the Bible passage quoted above) and explained that we have a "whatever it takes without violating our faith" approach to outreach at Crossline so that more and more people might come to faith in Christ. We are not hung up on nonessentials that put up unnecessary barriers to connection. We make ourselves open and available to people, find common connections—the human ones we all share and care deeply about—and build the bridge from where they are to the gospel.

One-dimensional religious approaches and insular spiritual communities are limiting to our outreach. I want to be like Jesus— *stretchy*. I want to imitate Paul—*free from the opinions of men* but a servant to all men. I want to be strong enough inside to enter the worlds of people not like me, see things from their points of view, understand their perspectives, and ask better questions. I want to serve them and help them any way I can, to create a human connection first that fosters some natural room for God to enter the relationship.

Being malleable makes the supernatural super *natural* for a variety of people around you. Being malleable is your way to help them access God. If you're a Kingdom person at the disposal of the indwelling Holy Spirit, that's your goal.

In a well-furnished kitchen there are not only crystal goblets and silver platters, but waste cans and compost buckets—some containers used to serve fine meals, others to take out the garbage. Become the kind of container God can use to present any and every kind of gift to his guests for their blessing.[11]

Holy Spirit,

I am present. I am ready. I am at your disposal for immediate use. I need you to remind me over and over how you dwell in me to work through me in the lives of others. I want to be more alert. I want to be seeking and sensing what you are doing wherever I am. Lead me from the inside out in my thoughts and attitudes. Specifically, guide my focus in the midst of life to be naturally fixed and locked in on the eternal. In faith, I ask that you keep my eternal radar continuously ON in the days to come.

Holy Spirit, produce your powerful fruit within me. I want to grow in all aspects of Jesus' character so that I can advance your purposes. Help me exhibit the fruit of love, joy, peace, forbearance, kindness, goodness, faithfulness, gentleness, and self-control to the people around me.

Holy Spirit, I am ready to be called spontaneously into a specific space with a specific person doing a specific thing as a follower. Speak to me, and I will be nimble like Philip to keep in step with you and serve another person you are preparing for me to interact with. Thank you that I don't have to try harder for you to use me; I just need to be available, always mindful of your working, flexible under your guidance, and adaptable within each opportunity.

Holy Spirit, empower me to influence people. Let your love for me stretch me to extend God's love to people where they are rather than demand that they stretch to me. Empower me to do whatever it takes without compromising my commitment to Jesus and his commands.

Let's go! Bring someone across my path. I am listening to you. In Jesus' name I pray. Amen.

PRAYERFUL TO GOD IN MY CONTEXT

I Am Seeking and Listening

THE DISTANCE FROM THE BEACHES of Normandy, France, to Berlin's Brandenburg Gate is approximately 844 miles. General George Patton's Third Army cut this exact path across Europe against the fiercest opposition ever encountered in modern warfare. This stunning and forceful advance took place over an astonishingly fast thirteen months of fighting. More poignantly, it was a lesson in retaking enemy territory that helped bring a decisive end to the agenda of an evil empire. From a military point of view, the march of the Third Army from a small beachfront opening in France to the Rhine and into Germany at least captures the imagination, and at most spawns admiration and respect.

"We are advancing constantly"[1] was Patton's famous charge to his men prior to hitting the beaches of Normandy—an expectation his men fulfilled. His troops joined the combat operations in Normandy in August 1944, and over the course of thirteen months, they reclaimed 10,000 miles of territory,[2] captured more than 300,000 prisoners of war,[3] and accelerated the liberation of Europe from Nazism and further holocaust.

Advancing armies continue to move forward because of men on the ground winning individual encounters.

The result? The taking of territory.

"Violent" Advance, Strong Weapon

Inviting the Holy Spirit into your encounters will undoubtedly be met by spiritual opposition. The advance of God's Kingdom in you and the taking of territory through you fits into a supernatural reality and panorama of spiritual warfare that is visceral and palpable. According to Jesus:

> From the time John the Baptist began preaching until now, the Kingdom of Heaven has been forcefully advancing, and violent people are attacking it.[4]

The advent of this campaign of eternal conquest is a reality check—more specifically, the reality of the Kingdom of God moving forward in force and every believer following in John the Baptist's footsteps in their own time and context. As members of this cosmic campaign, each of us has personal and private fields of battle we are called on to engage and win—for a family, a home, a neighborhood, a workplace; in a hospital room; against an injustice; or most significantly, for a soul. Wherever you see humanity living and breathing and working and playing, that is where God sends his men to advance his Kingdom agenda. Each battle is unique, with its own dynamics, spiritual terrain, and forces in play. Each man must perform his Kingdom duty in coordination with others in the Kingdom army at any given moment. The result? Demonic forces and worldly strongholds are displaced by individual soldiers bravely advancing with their weapons leveled at a target, directing fire downrange and eventually overtaking and occupying that territory for God.

If all that seems too Purple Heart–ish for your spiritual taste-buds, let the Word of God provide ultimate clarity and conviction about God's Kingdom advance in your world.

> We are human, but we don't wage war as humans do.
> We use God's mighty weapons, not worldly weapons, to
> knock down the strongholds of human reasoning and to
> destroy false arguments. We destroy every proud obstacle
> that keeps people from knowing God. We capture their
> rebellious thoughts and teach them to obey Christ. And
> after you have become fully obedient, we will punish
> everyone who remains disobedient.
>
> Look at the obvious facts. Those who say they belong
> to Christ must recognize that we belong to Christ as
> much as they do. I may seem to be boasting too much
> about the authority given to us by the Lord. But our
> authority builds you up; it doesn't tear you down. So I
> will not be ashamed of using my authority.[5]

God chooses to advance his Kingdom by delegating his spiritual authority to those in his service. These same people use the spiritual weapons he provides to win supernatural encounters because they have been given the authority to do so.

> God is strong, and he wants you strong. So take
> everything the Master has set out for you, well-made
> weapons of the best materials. And put them to use so

you will be able to stand up to everything the Devil throws your way. This is no weekend war that we'll walk away from and forget about in a couple of hours. This is for keeps, a life-or-death fight to the finish against the Devil and all his angels.

Be prepared. You're up against far more than you can handle on your own. Take all the help you can get, every weapon God has issued, so that when it's all over but the shouting you'll still be on your feet. Truth, righteousness, peace, faith, and salvation are more than words. Learn how to apply them. You'll need them throughout your life. God's Word is an *indispensable* weapon. In the same way, prayer is essential in this ongoing warfare. Pray hard and long. Pray for your brothers and sisters. Keep your eyes open. Keep each other's spirits up so that no one falls behind or drops out.[6]

- Prayer is the kinetic response (the energy) we deploy in spiritual battle.
- Prayer is an access point to the power of God.
- Prayer is the process by which spiritual armor is fitted onto our spirits.
- Prayer is the precious supply line of fuel that sustains a good offense when we engage in spiritual warfare.

So many Christ-following people know these truths intellectually but fail to exercise their spiritual authority experientially to win spiritual battles. That is why Jesus delegated his authority to his disciples and directed them to exercise their spiritual authority in the lives of others to advance the Kingdom of God. They went into the world they lived in and then lived out "your Kingdom come, your will be done," using their weapon of prayer with impunity and holy intent against unseen enemies. The Gospels record the supernatural victories that started happening—not through the professional ministers of the day but through the everyday believers in nonreligious spaces.

God's strategy for advance was pedestrian and powerful.

Later the Master selected seventy and sent them ahead of him in pairs to every town and place where he intended to go. He gave them this charge:

"What a huge harvest! And how few the harvest hands. So on your knees; ask the God of the Harvest to send harvest hands.

"On your way! But be careful—this is hazardous work. You're like lambs in a wolf pack. . . ."

The seventy came back triumphant. "Master, even the demons danced to your tune!"

Jesus said, "I know. I saw Satan fall, a bolt of lightning out of the sky. See what I've given you? Safe passage as you walk on snakes and scorpions, and protection from every assault of the Enemy. No one can put a hand on you. All the same, the great triumph is not in your authority over evil, but in God's authority over you and presence with you. Not what you do for God but what God does for you—that's the agenda for rejoicing."

At that, Jesus rejoiced, exuberant in the Holy Spirit. "I thank you, Father, Master of heaven and earth, that you hid these things from the know-it-alls and showed them to these innocent newcomers. Yes, Father, it pleased you to do it this way."[7]

What a scene! Father, Son, and Holy Spirit celebrating the triumph of Kingdom troops entering hostile environments and using spiritual weapons to take territory. Jesus saw followers understanding their identity, receiving Jesus' authority, and taking action in the midst of people that needed freedom, healing, and deliverance from the world, their flesh, and the devil. These new disciples were witnessing the difference between power and authority. Satan could only fall.

Praying with Spiritual Authority

On a snowy Black Friday, Michigan Avenue in downtown Chicago was packed with people getting a jump on their Christmas shopping. The atmosphere was magical but crowded. I was headed north toward my hotel with close to ten blocks of walking ahead of me as I approached a large intersection. The traffic light and the pedestrian crossing light were both red, and everyone at the intersection was at a standstill. A crowd began to gather on my side of the street until close to a hundred people were piled onto the corner, waiting for the light to change.

A few people decided to cross. As they did, others did too. I followed along until a loud whistle drew our attention to the middle of the street, where a traffic officer had one hand raised as the other hand waved us back to the corner to wait until the light turned green. In a split second, the whole group backed up to the corner. Not one pair of feet was on the street!

At first I said to myself, *Now* that *is power.* But then I looked at the officer, all decked out in her uniform—Chicago PD parka, hat, badge, and vest—standing tall in the middle of that busy intersection, and thought, *Now* that *is authority.*

What's the difference, you ask? If our group of one hundred people wanted to continue crossing the street against the traffic light, the police officer would have been physically powerless to stop us. But because she was vested with the authority of the City of Chicago, she didn't need to move an inch. All she had to do was blow that whistle and wave her hand, and we obeyed her command.

The same is true for any kind of referee in professional sports. Physically, many players are stronger than those officiating the game or match. But when it comes to a ruling on the field or court, a player's physical attributes are useless. The man or woman wearing the black-and-white uniform has been vested with authority by the league, and in the end, it's his or her ruling that is enforced, not the powerful player's.

You have authority delegated to you by Jesus. The Holy Spirit animates it through faith. Prayer conducts and directs it. God celebrates us using it.

God is clear on the spiritual authority you have. Honestly, are you? If you answered no, you're in good company. Many Christians don't understand how their spiritual authority in Christ actually works or how God's Word forcefully supports the believers' exercise of it. Many men know the Bible and understand intellectually that Jesus rules over all of creation, defeated death and Satan through his resurrection, and will triumph in the end. Those same men pray regularly, sincerely, and perhaps fervently as a discipline. They punctuate their prayers with "in Jesus' name," believing God has heard them, hopeful that God will consider their request and that if God so chooses, he will act. They are disciplined, but in the end, they are not a threat to evil, at least not in the way Jesus commissioned his followers.

Advancing the Kingdom requires understanding and exercising our spiritual authority.

God says: "If I am sending you under my authority, pray with my authority."

Jesus now called the Twelve and gave them authority and power to deal with all the demons and cure diseases. He commissioned them to preach the news of God's kingdom and heal the sick. He said, "Don't load yourselves up with equipment. Keep it simple; *you* are the equipment."[8]

This is what God calls us to:

- Suit up and show up.
- Don't overthink it.
- Don't look to the other guy. Don't compare yourself to another disciple.
- It's not about what you can do but what God can do through you.
- God's authority is your authority to be dangerous with goodness.
- Open your mouth and let people know that you have experienced God.
- Step into situations of need in God's authority and declare life, healing, salvation, freedom, and deliverance in his name.

Jesus was emphatic and confident in his followers having confidence in him! God's word to us today reflects it: "It doesn't matter if you are one of the Twelve or a part of the crowd. If you believe in and follow me, you are empowered to advance the Kingdom. Your own self-perception is officially overruled by my actual perception of you, your connection to my Son, my response to you as my own child, and my commission of you as a deputized ambassador of my Kingdom."

Filled with the Holy Spirit, the Twelve declared Jesus' authority over physical issues, spiritual oppression, and the salvation of souls. When they did this, an entire city began to hear about what these men were doing, made the connection to Jesus, and came to believe—thousands at a time. You can have a similar impact when you pray with spiritual authority within the rhythm and flow of everyday life in your community.

In Acts 3, Peter tells the curious religious leaders:

> "By faith in the name of Jesus, this man whom you see and know was made strong. It is Jesus' name and the faith that comes through him that has completely healed him, as you can all see."[9]

And in Acts 4, we read:

> Now as they observed the confidence of Peter and John and understood that they were uneducated and untrained men, they were amazed, and began to recognize them as having been with Jesus. And seeing the man who had been healed standing with them, they had nothing to say in reply. But when they had ordered them to leave the Council, they began to confer with one another, saying, "What shall we do with these men? For the fact that a noteworthy miracle has taken place through them is apparent to all who live in Jerusalem, and we cannot deny it. But so that it will not spread any further among the people, let us warn them to speak no longer to any man in this name." And when they had summoned them, they commanded them not to speak or teach at all in the name of Jesus.[10]

What Peter seems to imply is that the man was completely healed in Jesus' name out of the overflow of faith from Peter and John.

Peter and John's faith in *that* name, spoken in faith over a man they encountered, is a good model for how God's man exercises his spiritual authority. I would love to think that somewhere in this dialogue Peter added, "I don't know what else to tell you." That simple? Yes. Jesus delegated to him his authority and sent him out, so he prayed in that authority and left the results to God.

Kingdom advanced.

God says: "If I fully define you in Christ, you are free to pray with the full authority of Christ."

> I also pray that you will understand the incredible greatness of God's power for us who believe him. This is the same mighty power that raised Christ from the dead and seated him in the place of honor at God's right hand in the heavenly realms. Now he is far above any ruler or authority or power or leader or anything else—not only in this world but also in the world to come. God has put all things under the authority of Christ and has made him head over all things for the benefit of the church. . . .
>
> For he raised us from the dead along with Christ and seated us with him in the heavenly realms because we are united with Christ Jesus.[11]

Self-perception determines identity and directly impacts how we approach prayer in any given situation. This is the reason behind the apostle Paul's focus on identity and his deep desire for the Ephesian believers to understand who they were in Christ. Specifically, he wanted them to internalize that their identity in Christ was synonymous with great power and authority over demonic spirits and that Jesus was raised, seated above *all* created beings in *all* realms, and put in charge over *all* things.

We are not just connected to him relationally. We are connected to him positionally, which changes everything about how we operate as a follower *right now*. "Seated us with him" means we *share* his position of authority and can exercise that same authority in prayer. Remember who you are and, in faith, act in that identity in prayer.

When God's perception of you prevails, you will pray with spiritual authority.

God says: "If I make a promise, hold me to it and apply it in prayer."

> And I tell you that you are Peter, and on this rock I
> will build my church, and the gates of Hades will not
> overcome it. I will give you the keys of the kingdom of
> heaven; whatever you bind on earth will be bound in
> heaven, and whatever you loose on earth will be loosed in
> heaven.[12]

The "gates" of a city in Jesus' time were where the elders met and the agenda for city governance was legislated and passed. Jesus is telling us that hell (the gates of Hades) has an agenda. But as my friend Dr. Tony Evans often says, for every evil gate, there is a Kingdom key. The holders of those keys who "loose" the agenda of the Kingdom of heaven against the gates of hades and prevail are none other than me, you, and every person alive on earth who names Jesus as their King and Savior. Or at least we are supposed to be. It is vital for Christians to see that in the very first mention of this new community Jesus would form called "the church," he explained that its primary purpose is to thwart hell's "gates" with God's Kingdom purposes. The church (filled with individuals who believe) would be given Kingdom keys to unlock every evil gate to accomplish its purpose. In other words, hell's agenda is threatened when God's people exercise their spiritual authority and use the Kingdom keys to bust open the gates. But how?

Answer: by declarative prayer that Jesus termed *binding and loosing*. While those words may sound strange to us, every Jew hearing Jesus say them would have heard rabbis declare people "bound" to or "loosed" from a particular law of Moses. But in a new twist for a new community, Jesus, as its head Rabbi, delegated the authority to bind and loose to the new community he was forming. Specifically, he gave spiritual authority to followers to *allow or forbid* in his name. To bind something was to forbid it, and to loose it was to allow it. His followers did not need rabbinical status to execute God's will. Since followers were united fully to Jesus, they were also united fully to his authority. This is exactly what you see transpire over and over again in the book of Acts when the Holy Spirit came upon believers. They used this delegated authority to bind hell's agenda and loose God's Kingdom in multiple expressions by declaring Jesus' authority in specific situations.

God is clear about the authority the church has to declare in prayer what is no longer going to be allowed and what activity will be permitted according to his will. The Kingdom advances when Kingdom men act on Jesus' promise in prayer, but as long as the church is ignorant of its authority, hell breathes easier.

The lesson? *Great victories over evil agendas await those who declare God's agenda.*

> Very truly I tell you, whoever believes in me will do the works I have been doing, and they will do even greater things than these, because I am going to the Father. And I will do whatever you ask in my name, so that the Father may be glorified in the Son. You may ask me for anything in my name, and I will do it.[13]

Key words? "Whoever believes . . . will do." It is a promise and an expectation. Jesus has perfect clarity for how belief in him should result in greater works for him. His statement is backed up with a direct encouragement to take him up on it *through proactively praying* for those greater works to be done in his name and for his glory. Have you ever taken Jesus up on his promise? Is it your desire to be ushered into the greater works of Jesus planned specifically for you to do in your context? Do you desire to glorify God by allowing him to use you in supernatural ways? If the answer is yes, then Jesus directs you to *let him know that you know* his promise. The Holy Spirit is waiting.

Apply your spiritual authority in prayer and ask God to do what he promised.

God says: "The way I told you to pray is direct and authoritative; pray that way!"

This, then, is how you should pray: "Our Father in heaven, hallowed be your name, your kingdom come, your will be done, on earth as it is in heaven. Give us today our daily bread. And forgive us our debts, as we also have forgiven our debtors. And lead us not into temptation, but deliver us from the evil one."[14]

My friend J. P. Jones, a theology professor at Biola University, shared some insight on this prayer with me as we were discussing an upcoming sermon. He pointed out something important I'd never noticed before:

Jesus instructs us to pray using the imperative when directing our requests to God. This is the strongest form of communication. In fact, if it were addressed to anyone else, we would assume the addressee is being commanded to do

*the requests mentioned. But since we are never in position to
exercise authority over God, we can only infer that Jesus is
telling us of our unique position of asking God to do what he is
able to do and our expectation that it will be done. Our prayers
release God to act! It's as if God is telling us, "Just say the word!"*

Prayer puts your faith into action by releasing what God has
already said he wants in your life. Listen to the apostle John coach
believers in prayer, helping them to pray with authority and confidence, knowing that God will do what he has already purposed to do.

My purpose in writing is simply this: that you who
believe in God's Son will know beyond the shadow of a
doubt that you have eternal life, the reality and not the
illusion. And how bold and free we then become in his
presence, freely asking according to his will, sure that he's
listening. And if we're confident that he's listening, we
know that what we've asked for is as good as ours.[15]

If God is for what you are asking, then be direct, be bold—ask
in the imperative!

- Move, Lord, to save.
- Move, Lord, to heal.
- Glorify yourself in this situation.
- Destroy the devil's works.
- Redeem this tragedy.
- Provide for my needs, Lord.
- Restrict evil.
- Release Kingdom power.
- Bind all lies.
- Dispatch truth through the Holy Spirit.

- Guard the minds and hearts of these little ones.
- Open the door for your Word.
- Save my coworker.
- Deliver peace that passes all understanding.
- Fill me with the Holy Spirit.
- Your Kingdom come.
- Rule in this space.
- Bind division.
- Bring unity.

Prayer is a spiritual tool for relationship with God. It is also our most potent weapon.

When we pray, sometimes we are the tip of the spear—leading an assault against forces opposing God's fullest will or presence. Other times we are the needed breakthrough force that turns the tide—showing up at a specific moment to provide power and relief through prayer. Sometimes we are the one to vanquish the enemy, projecting our fullest authority rooted in our identity, sending him and all demonic powers back into the dark dimension from which they came.

Battles are about to begin, and as you see situations or encounters on the horizon, send prayers ahead like preinvasion artillery softening the soil for the beach landing. If you find yourself in a messy or complicated situation, ask others to lay down a covering of prayer over you like suppression fire that allows you to move freely without opposition or achieve a new perspective in the situation. But if you find yourself depressed or anxious, and those feelings are controlling you, you may need to rise in the authority Jesus has given you, declare your position, and exercise your spiritual authority over principalities, powers, or spiritual wickedness in the heavenly realms.[16]

We are constantly advancing.

Mighty God of Heaven,

I recognize and receive my position and seat with Christ. You have called me into your Kingdom and given me authority to advance your Kingdom everywhere I find myself. You have given me Kingdom keys to unlock your will and block evil agendas. You have given me your authority to bind and to loose.

Thank you for my position. Thank you for the privilege to pray, right now, in obedience to who you say I am in Christ. By your authority and in your name, I ask you to take action in my life and through my life:

In my heart, I bind doubt and fear and loose faith and power. I bind any sickness of character and loose healing and freedom.

In my relationships and family, I bind division and chaos and loose unity and grace. In Jesus' name, I pray for resentment to cease and forgiveness to flourish.

In my church, I bind sin and loose holiness. I bind division and loose unity. In Jesus' name, I bind all the schemes of the devil and loose harvest through your people in the power of the Holy Spirit.

On the soil upon which I stand, I bind all curses and attacks against me and I loose the resurrection power of Jesus, in his mighty name. I ask for the presence of the Holy Spirit and for salvation, miracles, and justice.

In Jesus' name, I declare my identity in Christ, my covering by his blood, and my authority over all powers of the evil one.

In Jesus' name, I declare his victory, his Kingdom come, and his will be done for his glory. Amen.

FAITHFUL TO GOD IN MY CONTEXT

I Commit without Knowing

IT IS CALLED PROXIMITY FLYING, and it is one of the most dangerous sports in the world. It is a form of BASE jumping that, at its top levels, means strapping into a nylon suit, intentionally placing yourself on a cliff (usually in the world's highest mountain ranges or fjords), and leaping off for the purpose of experiencing raw (non-vessel) human flight.[1] Maybe you've seen a YouTube video of these guys who look like flying squirrels paralleling a mountain side or cliff at terminal velocity and, as you watch them, your stomach starts reacting. The first reaction is *the leap*.

Is it an act of faith? One hundred percent.

These men *commit without knowing* (before the fact) if they will survive, and they complete this exercise of faith with *the action* of jumping off a cliff. They are putting their faith and trust in a number of factors.

- **Their training**—Most are expert skydivers and BASE jumpers with years of experience.
- **Their wingsuit**—They use a specially engineered nylon costume that fills the suit's baffles with air within one second of a jump and turns them rigid.[2]
- **Their physical skills**—An expert wingsuit pilot understands the physics of body positions, glide ratios, subtle shifts in shoulder and arm movements, and how all of that works with air speeds exceeding one hundred miles per hour.
- **Their preplanning**—Before they take that leap, they have mapped out their "lines" of descent, which can span miles from their launch point.
- **Their fail-safe**—A wingsuit is not enough for a safe landing, so every pilot utilizes a parachute for touchdown.

So yes, these men are strongly persuaded that what has happened to hundreds of men since the sport originated in the 1990s will not happen to them. They are confident and convinced they are not going to die when they take the big leap. They have to be to engage such risk. Yes, the stakes are extremely high. Yes, the margin for error is razor thin. Yes, the rewards are unforgettable.

Every risk a human being takes starts with hope.

I will never be a proximity flyer. While the sport may seem an extreme example of faith, in actuality, I am remarkably similar to these insanely brave men—and so are you.

Forget jumping off a fjord in Norway for a moment, and think about how acts of faith are built into the fabric of our everyday existence and rhythms. You head to the airport and get on a plane. Can you say, before the fact, that your plane *will land* at your destination? Of course you can't. However, like these wingsuit pilots, you are *very persuaded* it will. You are putting your faith in the fact that the pilot has extensive training and experience. You are putting your faith in the laws of physics that will produce the lift you need to fly. You are putting your faith in the likelihood that a flock of geese won't fly into your plane's massive jet engines. You are putting your faith in the assembly, for example, of your Boeing 737 aircraft, which consists of 367,000 separate parts put together by human beings.[3] Additionally, you are putting your faith in the idea that all those parts and systems are going to work flawlessly from takeoff to landing. So what do you do? You complete your faith with the action of stepping into the plane, buckling up, and letting it take off with you inside it. Like me, you are very persuaded you are going to land, but you *cannot know that before the fact.*

Been to the doctor lately? A doctor listens, looks, runs a few tests, and recommends a therapy or medicine that will address the presenting issues. You can't know in advance whether those recommendations will work, but you believe your doctor was well trained at medical school and has been educated on the efficacy of the prescribed medicine. You take the pill, don't you?

Drive your car to work today? It never entered your mind that you might not make it there, did it? We get to work most every day without incident, take the kids to practice, and drive to Grandma's expecting to get from where we are to where we need to be. Same as BASE jumping, flying on a plane, or going to the doctor. While we may be convinced that other drivers won't drink before they drive, will be alert and drive safely, and will obey the law, we know many won't and don't. We trust the roads will be safe, the weather will be manageable, and we won't blow a tire. None of those factors stops us and—rightly persuaded—we start the car, put it in gear, and take off, completing our act of faith.

The question you have to ask yourself is this: Are you persuaded to risk it all for God?

Just as it was with the wingsuit pilot's big leap, the stakes are extremely high. However, unlike what lay before the cliff-jumping man in a squirrel suit, here God has eliminated the margin for error. And most importantly, the experience of an unforgettable reward will be *forever*. Don't believe me. Believe Jesus.

> If you try to hang on to your life, you will lose it. But if you give up your life for my sake and for the sake of the Good News, you will save it.[4]

Get the picture here? Jesus is talking about hanging on or letting go. Playing it safe or taking that risk. Unforgettable regret or an unforgettable experience. It all comes down to moments on the precipices of life and a choice. God says: "Well? What's it going to be?"

Here we go.

Intentional and Intelligent Abandon

The Holy Spirit says: "There is no such thing as the 'safe' Christian life."

This is hard for followers who like predictability, comfort, or control. But we are commanded to engage in intentional and intelligent risk-taking as part of our relationship with God. The Bible refers to this as being faithful. In fact, faithfulness is something the Holy Spirit develops in you. He wants to make you the sort of person who will commit to the person, promise, or plan of God *without* knowing the outcome and will then demonstrate that commitment by taking an action in faith.

This is not a blind leap of faith. In fact, it is the exact opposite. In life, we are persuaded to take all kinds of risks because the hope of the outcome is worth it to us; this extends to our faith lives. Faithfulness looks like moments where you stop contemplating action and start acting toward God's will or desire in a given situation—again, without knowing for sure what's going to happen. These moments are actually *preplanned* by God for us to risk stepping into.

> He creates each of us by Christ Jesus to join him in the
> work he does, the good work he has gotten ready for us to
> do, work we had better be doing.[5]

You are created specifically for *your* particular place in time and history. The Holy Spirit will prompt us, saying, *"Join me right now in what I am doing. You are my partner in this situation."* In that moment, we will do one of two things: we will either risk in faith or we will retreat. And because God has prearranged and customized these moments ahead of time for us, he has specific feelings about the nature and direction of our choices in these moments.

> "But my righteous one will live by faith. And I take no
> pleasure in the one who shrinks back."
> But we do not belong to those who shrink back and
> are destroyed, but to those who have faith and are saved.[6]

God takes our choice to be faithful in the moment and risk for his purposes very personally.

You are set apart for God's purposes.

> But my righteous one . . .
> HEBREWS 10:38, NIV

God is watching his sons and daughters, just like any good father. He's following us with his eye. As we will see, he tracked his own Son, and God is tracking his sons in Christ right now. In the moments when we have the opportunity to participate in what God is doing around us, he leans in, keenly interested to see us influence others by doing the good he calls us to do.

In the passages below, God tracks and responds to the choices of the sons of Israel. God tracks and publicly reflects upon Jesus' ministry on earth with the disciples. Watch how he watches.

> For the vineyard of the LORD of hosts is the house
> of Israel and the men of Judah His delightful plant.
> Thus He looked for justice, but behold, bloodshed; for
> righteousness, but behold, a cry of distress.[7]

> Jesus took Peter and the brothers, James and John, and
> led them up a high mountain. His appearance changed
> from the inside out, right before their eyes. Sunlight
> poured from his face. His clothes were filled with light.
> Then they realized that Moses and Elijah were also there
> in deep conversation with him.
>   Peter broke in, "Master, this is a great moment!
> What would you think if I built three memorials here
> on the mountain—one for you, one for Moses, one for
> Elijah?"
>   While he was going on like this, babbling, a light-
> radiant cloud enveloped them, and sounding from deep
> in the cloud a voice: "This is my Son, marked by my love,
> focus of my delight. Listen to him."[8]

In one instance, God is looking for the family resemblance and finds it missing. In the other he sees the sum of Jesus' choices and tells the disciples to keep listening to him! He is pleased with what he sees Jesus doing.

Is he pleased with what he sees me doing?

It reminds me of when my kids would leave for school and I would let them almost get to the car before shouting, "Hey!"—getting them to all turn around at the same time. Once they all had me locked in their sights, I would then say, "Remember, you are a Luck, and Lucks love God and help people." They were not just anybody's children; they were *my* children! I was tracking their character and their choices, especially under the ever-present and powerful pressure of the middle- and high-school years. I was keenly interested in their choices and their character. I never stopped giving them that reminder because, while I may not have been able to follow them around, I wanted them to know who they were. And when you know who you are, you know what to do in the critical moments. The converse of that is true as well. If you don't know who you are, you will be unsure of what to do and will instead do what is emotionally expedient, comfortable, or culturally acceptable. I believe that urge as a father came directly from our heavenly Father and his own personal drive for a family identity.

In a very real and forceful way, God is saying, *"You are not just anybody who can do anything. You are called as a member of this family to bring a Spirit-empowered choice and action into this situation."* And when the Holy Spirit delivers that message, we rejoice and take pride in representing our Father.

In your next Kingdom moment, God says: "You're a member of my family."

You take risks others don't take.

. . . my righteous one will live by faith.
HEBREWS 10:38, NIV

Our dominant filter for personal and public decision-making looks like intelligent and intentional abandon in the direction of God's desires. This faith-filter has a unique feature: it does not account for what the outcome may be and is unconcerned with the consequences. When you consider the cast of men and women in the hall of faith of Hebrews 11, the common denominators are straightforward, strong, and consistent:

- Each man or woman wrestled with a choice: God or self-preservation.
- Each man or woman was persuaded—regardless of the outcome—that the choice for God would be rewarded in this life or in eternity.
- Each man or woman committed by taking a step of faith.
- Each man or woman had a right view of God and decided to risk big.

Under the pressure of the choice, their lives in God reflected their view of God. That meant that while the faith choice in the moment may have appeared counterintuitive or they may not have fully comprehended the "why" behind it, they knew God was just, good, wise, and loving and that he had the power to redeem their choice for his glory. This was their distinct and powerful driver.

The fundamental fact of existence is that this trust in God, this faith, is the firm foundation under everything that makes life worth living. It's our handle on what we can't see. The act of faith is what distinguished our ancestors, set them above the crowd.[9]

Don't miss this. Being faithful in a given moment—risking toward our eternal hopes—is what set these men and women apart. What they modeled for us is meant for us, calling us forward into a new and stronger commitment to risk hard while we still have time.

You are living out an important generational link in God's magnificent family chain spanning all the generations of his righteous ones. The Holy Spirit wants you to see just how important you are in the overarching tale of God's eternal Kingdom story.

Do you see what this means—all these pioneers who blazed the way, all these veterans cheering us on? It means we'd better get on with it. Strip down, start running— and never quit! No extra spiritual fat, no parasitic sins. Keep your eyes on *Jesus*, who both began and finished this race we're in. Study how he did it. Because he never lost sight of where he was headed—that exhilarating finish in and with God—he could put up with anything along the way: Cross, shame, whatever. And now he's *there*, in the place of honor, right alongside God. When you find yourselves flagging in your faith, go over that story again, item by item, that long litany of hostility he plowed through. *That* will shoot adrenaline into your souls![10]

You don't call people to spiritual discipline unless there is real temptation to be undisciplined in faith. You don't say "never quit" unless there are days when believers will feel like giving up the faith journey. You don't mention low points in the faith journey unless God's people experience them here on earth. You don't call people to a singular focus unless the tendency is to drift some—or even a lot.

Without discipline, all of us will be pulled away from our callings. Even so, we have a tried-and-true way of finding our spiritual power and resolve again. We focus on Jesus, his finish on our behalf, the courageous choices he made for us at the expense of his own comfort, and the endurance he showed to the end. His willingness to risk it all *for us* breeds a willingness in his servants to keep risking it all *for him* to the end.

That's the process—risk for him in today's moments, wake up tomorrow, renew your focus, and keep risking faithfulness in the new opportunities. Do this one day at a time until you ultimately transition to *that* day when Jesus says:

> Well done, my good and faithful servant. You have been faithful in handling this small amount, so now I will give you many more responsibilities. Let's celebrate together![11]

In your next Kingdom moment, God says: "Risk it all for me."

You know what pleases God—shrinking back from opportunity isn't it.

> "I take no pleasure in the one who shrinks back." But we do not belong to those who shrink back and are destroyed, but to those who have faith and are saved.
> **HEBREWS 10:38-39, NIV**

Like a boxer who has his opponent on the ropes, we press on in the Kingdom fight until a judgment, outcome, or deliverance is reached—until all of God's purposes are fulfilled in a given situation. We don't "sort of" step into the opportunities God has thoughtfully orchestrated. Knowing he is with us gives us a proactive confidence and longing to see his desires come to pass.

This does not mean we are obnoxious, anxious, or manipulative in Jesus' name. It simply means we enter and remain connected in the opportunity God has opened up until the Holy Spirit secures God's desire, relieves us of our involvement, or releases us to advance God's next opportunity. Risking for God is not a fleeting or weak event. Whenever God is involved, there is a process of faith that requires persistence, patience, and trust in his plan, which usually looks a lot different from our own plan.

All followers of Jesus have episodes in their faith journey in which some of the most powerful and life-changing opportunities God provided didn't look like they came from God at all—at least not at first. In these instances, believers are placed in uncomfortable, inconvenient, or extended situations where they may start to doubt. God, however, is always behind the scenes! More importantly, God is bigger than the apparent obstacles or perceived messiness that tempt them to bail out right away. And that's the point.

The Holy Spirit says: "It is never God's will for you to run from a problem."

Chew on that one a little. Let it sink in. Digest it. Is it any wonder that, in Scripture, God seems to be upset with his people on the regular? His people know exactly who he is and what he is capable of. They have seen him work in mighty ways, but they quickly forget! The Bible is a record of God's people being delivered, forgetting, being distracted by their circumstances, losing faith, and making bad choices out of fear, and then God reteaching them that *he is over everything, sees everything, and can do anything*! Thus, it is completely consistent for him to feel this kind of disappointment and displeasure. Picture a father ready to catch his child as she jumps into the pool. Dad knows who he is in this moment, knows what he is capable of. But his child is focused on the water, not on Dad! She is paralyzed by her fear and steps back from an amazing thrill and a strong catch. Dad is disappointed; he wanted to share a special moment, and his child is holding back.

In the opportunities God gives us, we have a choice. We can either focus on all the reasons not to enter into it or we can focus on God, who has called us into it. Choose one, and it leads to regret and regret only in the end. Choose the other, and well, a couple of explosive things happen.

> It's impossible to please God apart from faith. And why? Because anyone who wants to approach God must believe both that he exists *and* that he cares enough to respond to those who seek him.[12]

First, our faith ignites God's pleasure, like throwing a match on gas-soaked wood. Whooooshhh! He gets lit up! Second, our risks for God's purposes bring a *response* from God. In other words, he *moves*.

In your next Kingdom moment, God says: "Go ahead and see what happens."

Doors of Opportunity

Being faithful in your context means seizing opportunities from the Holy Spirit in the flow of your life. If you miss a temporal opportunity—one where there is no forever consequence to it—you may regret it later. But if you miss an eternal opportunity, that is another thing altogether because when you reflect back from eternity's vantage point, you realize time only heads in a forward direction. There is no going back. You missed it. This is precisely why Jesus encouraged and warned his followers to live with a disciplined sense of urgency, knowing that life on earth is a fleeting and costly preparation for eternity. His clear message: choose the pain of Spirit-empowered discipline now, because the pain of regret is ten times worse!

[Jesus said,] We need to be energetically at work for the One who sent me here, working while the sun shines. When night falls, the workday is over.[13]

Don't hoard treasure down here where it gets eaten by moths and corroded by rust or—worse!—stolen by burglars. Stockpile treasure in heaven, where it's safe from moth and rust and burglars. It's obvious, isn't it? The place where your treasure is, is the place you will most want to be, and end up being.[14]

Jesus strongly coaches us to make choices aligned with where we will end up and what will count there versus where we are now and what will die with us here.

The Holy Spirit says: "Live for the ultimate, not the immediate."

Let us not become weary in doing good, for at the proper time we will reap a harvest if we do not give up. Therefore, as we have opportunity, let us do good to all people, especially to those who belong to the family of believers.[15]

Doors of opportunity don't align with your feelings.

Let us not become weary in doing good, for at the proper time we will reap a harvest if we do not give up.

GALATIANS 6:9, NIV

One difference between a toddler and an adult is that one is ruled by feelings and the other can see the big picture revealed only by maturity and perspective. Adults are just big little kids when they get hungry, angry, lonely, or tired. Count me among them! We lose sight of the big picture sometimes. And God undoubtedly knows we get tired and on some days we just—well—*can't*. But sometimes, in the midst of the normal ups and downs, we play the feelings card, as in "Not now, but maybe next time" or "I can't meet everybody's needs; there are simply too many" or "Right now, I need some me time." Those could all be valid responses to situations that are calling for your presence, involvement, and faith-filled risk for the Kingdom of God. At the time, they feel completely justified, and you could make a case for each one—*to yourself*.

The problem is that what we tell ourselves first in the moment is usually a response based on our feelings rather than a response based on faith. I am very prone to this, but then the Holy Spirit reminds me, "You *could* do that, but if you do what shows love for Jesus and love for people *right now*, you won't regret it later." I call this boomerang obedience. My initial response is less than Spirit-filled, but then I am gently reminded of my identity and where that identity tells me to place my energy. Hopefully, I will respond to eternity's call, not my flesh's. This is real-world obedience that impacts my world. There has to be some pain and cost attached to it or else it wouldn't require faith. There must be the losing of my life for his sake to secure my eternal life. I'm still working on this one. Are you?

> At the time, discipline isn't much fun. It always feels like it's going against the grain. Later, of course, it pays off big-time, for it's the well-trained who find themselves mature in their relationship with God.[16]

The Holy Spirit says: "You can choose the pain of discipline or the pain of regret."

Big-time payoff? I will choose the pain of discipline, Holy Spirit.

Doors of opportunity will time out.

> Therefore, as we have opportunity . . .
>
> GALATIANS 6:10, NIV

God says he will introduce situations custom-engineered for our Kingdom involvement, but they're called "moments" in time for a reason. Doors open and close. People are available until they become unavailable. Needs show themselves and recede. Family or friends are in crisis and open to truth like never before, but after their needs are met, the gift of desperation is left unopened. Texts asking if you have time for coffee this week become visible and then fall into your digital ocean of messages. You are in seat 19A, and the person in seat 19B on your three-hour flight is going through a major life trauma under the surface. You have exactly what he needs, but when you land, you will board different connecting flights.

> *opportunity (n.): a favorable juncture of circumstances; a good chance for advancement or progress*[17]*; an amount of time or a situation in which something can be done*[18]

It may not look like it, but circumstances have been sovereignly arranged by God for seizing. But to capture the moment for God, you must take possession of it personally, being faithful to the opportunity God provides by recognizing it will not be there forever.

> Use your heads as you live and work among outsiders.
> Don't miss a trick. Make the most of every opportunity.
> Be gracious in your speech. The goal is to bring out the
> best in others in a conversation, not put them down, not
> cut them out.[19]

I want to come and stay awhile, if the Lord will let me. In the meantime, I will be staying here at Ephesus until the Festival of Pentecost. There is a wide-open door for a great work here, although many oppose me.[20]

The Holy Spirit says: "When you see and sense it—seize it for the Kingdom."

Doors of opportunity require character.

Let us do good to all people.
GALATIANS 6:10, NIV

God wants "good" to flow from you into the opportunity God has given you—a situation or a person's life. This "good" is one thing with a variety of possible expressions. One reason so many opportunities are missed and feelings trump faith in the moment is that there is not enough "good" stored up *inside* to flow *outside*. You cannot give away what you do not possess in any given moment. One solution is to make sure you are regularly loading up on the "good" within so you have a supply to give away when called upon.

A tree is identified by its fruit. If a tree is good, its fruit will be good. If a tree is bad, its fruit will be bad. You brood of snakes! How could evil men like you speak what is good and right? For whatever is in your heart determines what you say. A good person produces good things from the treasury of a good heart, and an evil person produces evil things from the treasury of an evil heart.[21]

Conduct in any moment is an expression of the substance of your inner character.

Fruit reflects the source. Apple trees make apples. Mango trees make mangoes. The Holy Spirit produces goodness. The source for your character on any given day will be reflected in your conduct that day. Picture a treasury or storage facility receiving regular deposits of gold that begin to create a surplus. Practically, this means a proactive filling of the Holy Spirit—the producer of "good" fruit—daily. It means you refuel your mind, heart, and soul (the character trifecta) with full helpings of God's Word on a daily basis. It also means prayer as worship and worship as prayer to seal what has been deposited into a commitment for that day. Lock the vault! These opportunities to fill up on God and his goodness precede the unlocking of your treasury, the overflow of God pouring forth his goodness in any given moment. And because Satan knows the power on the other side of this "storing up," he will seek to disrupt that, work to hurry you up, attempt to tie you down digitally, or move to panic you professionally. Sound familiar?

Treat your character like a gas tank and fill 'er up so the throttle of your character has good fuel to draw on when called upon.

> I pray that God, the source of hope, will fill you
> completely with joy and peace because you trust in him.
> Then you will overflow with confident hope through the
> power of the Holy Spirit.
>   I am fully convinced, my dear brothers and sisters,
> that you are full of goodness. You know these things so
> well you can teach each other all about them. Even so,
> I have been bold enough to write about some of these
> points, knowing that all you need is this reminder.[22]

The Holy Spirit says: "Fill up! Then you can faithfully pour out in the moment."

Being faithful in your context means being alert to the opportunities God is orchestrating. They are all around you, disguised within routine places and people. Remember this: the opportunities that look small might have big, unseen backstories that need to be tapped by a small but meaningful "You good?" and a patient waiting around for an answer or a second question. Don't forget: the doors that feel big, obvious, and overwhelming don't affect God the same way. He knows your limitations. Simply be faithful and risk being a good link in a good chain that leads to God's glory. Be brave. Forget predictable, comfortable, and safe—the Kingdom is fluid, dynamic, unpredictable, and full of twists and turns. God's doors of opportunity are definitely mysterious, but they are not unrecognizable because of the indwelling Holy Spirit. Stay available to the Holy Spirit. Stay prayerful in the Spirit on all occasions. Stay faithful, and enter the moment prepared for you.

Big God. Big purpose. Big hope. Big faith. Big risks.

Leap!

Holy Spirit,

You want to use me, and I want to be used today. Fill me, lead me, and empower me to recognize doors of opportunity from you and walk through them in faith. Make living by faith my way to be, my way to believe, my way to behave. I am yours, and I want to risk it all for your purposes, just as Jesus risked it all for me. I don't want to miss one moment appointed by you, so help me to discipline my spirit to say yes when my feelings are saying no. Teach me that each moment is the moment of faith—being obedient when I don't feel like it. I declare, in Jesus' name, those future moments won in advance for your purposes.

Open my eyes to the Kingdom intersections of my life with people. I look forward to entering them. Give me discernment to know how to enter through a Kingdom door. If I am not seeing it, push me through if you must, for I want to be faithful. And when I am in, Holy Spirit, guide me and reveal your goodness through me. I want to overflow my confident hope in Jesus in every dimension of my life without thought to man but instead with all my thoughts on the future. I want to hear, "Well done, good and faithful servant"—so I declare your Kingdom come in me and through me as often as you will. Thank you that I have what I ask because I ask according to your Word and will. In Jesus' name, let the doors open! Amen.

PART III

OVERFLOWING WORKS

7

SETTING THE
HOLY SPIRIT LOOSE

I Am a Fire Starter

IT WAS A GLOBALLY EXPERIENCED RELEASE OF POWER.
The sound of the explosion was heard up to three thousand miles
away. That is on-the-ground intel following the Krakatoa volcano
eruption in Indonesia in 1883. More scientifically, the Volcanic
Explosivity Index (VEI) was a 6, which rates the explosion as
"colossal" or "unusually and impressively large." The scale of
impact, the range of impact, and the degree to which this volcano
affected the globe has not been matched in modern times.

- Volcanic ash from the explosion fell on the decks of ships
  1,600 miles away.

- The explosion event itself could be heard across an area
  larger than one-third of the earth's surface, beginning

in Indonesia and echoing as far away as Australia and Rodrigues Island, located a thousand miles east of Madagascar. A "distant roar of cannons" was how people described the sound.

- Ash rose more than fifty miles into the atmosphere.

- Spectacular "red sky" sunsets were reported in the United States and Europe for the next three years due to sunlight scattering off aerosolized ash.

- A volcanic "dust veil" acted as a solar radiation filter that caused global temperatures to drop and changed worldwide climatology for the next five years.[1]

Purest shock. Strongest awe. Impact seen and felt after release. The scientific principle behind all the volcano's effects is connected to the displacement volume of an explosive event. In everyday terms, we refer to this as a "blast zone." Krakatoa's unique force was unusually large because of a unique event within the volcano that occurred during the "normal" explosion.

Something *got inside it.*

As the volcano's walls began to rupture after the first two explosions, ocean water entered the magmatic chambers, creating the conditions for a *phreatomagmatic event.* This is a volcanic eruption caused by contact between magma and groundwater in which the water, gases, and steam combine to create an explosion. This was the secret power behind Krakatoa's unusual force and incredible displacement power.[2] The mother of all pressure cookers was created, contained, and then launched its payload skyward at the moment when the power inside overcame the earthen ceiling above.

The result: a super-explosion that literally rocked the world.

What Has Gotten into You?

What do phreatomagmatic volcanic events, Krakatoa, the Holy Spirit, and rocking the world have to do with you?

Everything.

As the Holy Spirit gets inside us and replaces our self-perceptions with our identities in Christ as his salt, his light, and his aroma, our energies get redirected. We are moved to become less available to our impulses and needs while becoming increasingly available to God's purposes. We fully identify with Christ, receiving and walking in the spiritual authority he delegated to us, making full use of it through prayer in the spaces and places we find ourselves. We commit to God's purposes without assurances of the outcome and put that commitment to the test by taking specific action. As we cooperate with the Holy Spirit in these ways, we see that the release of the Holy Spirit through us is often counterintuitive and requires trust. It is helpful to look again at how Jesus predicted the displacement factor of his followers under the influence of the Holy Spirit:

> "What you'll get is the Holy Spirit. And when the Holy Spirit comes on you, you will be able to be my witnesses in Jerusalem, all over Judea and Samaria, even to the ends of the world."
>
> These were his last words. As they watched, he was taken up and disappeared in a cloud. They stood there, staring into the empty sky. Suddenly two men appeared—in white robes! They said, "You Galileans!—why do you just stand here looking up at an empty sky? This very Jesus who was taken up from among you to heaven will come as certainly—and mysteriously—as he left."[3]

A turning point in world history loomed. Something was about to happen that would reverberate out of Jerusalem and be felt in the private and public worlds of every follower who would be filled. Jesus' leaving was the first and necessary explosion the disciples *had to feel*. The walls of their personal expectations— that Jesus would build a literal, physical kingdom on earth— would finally collapse when he ascended, making way inwardly for the deeply flooding entry of the Holy Spirit. In other words, an emotional low in the disciples and a power from on high were about to coalesce, establishing the perfect conditions for a Spirit-induced super-explosion of power and supernatural purpose.

The boiling hopes, the magmatic expectations, and the powerful attachments of the disciples over the last three years were ruptured *intentionally* by God, leaving a gaping hole of opportunity *in them*. Soon after Jesus' promise, the fissures opened, and the Holy Spirit flooded every cavity of their souls with inner assurance and a powerful anointing for the purpose of overflow. Suddenly, living water inundated their souls, rapidly mixing with and making perfect sense of all the anticipations, prospects, and probabilities of their relationship with Jesus. All the spiritual dots were connecting, and the lid on their willingness to be used for God's purpose was blown off. The initial explosion of spiritual energy created by the Holy Spirit was so powerful that those who witnessed this transformation of Jesus' followers were at a complete loss.

Someone had to explain this spectacle of men transformed by the explosion.

That's when Peter stood up and, backed by the other eleven, spoke out with bold urgency: "Fellow Jews, all of you who are visiting Jerusalem, listen carefully and get this story straight. These people aren't drunk as some of you suspect. They haven't had time to get drunk— it's only nine o'clock in the morning. This is what the prophet Joel announced would happen:

'In the Last Days,' God says,
'I will pour out my Spirit
   on every kind of people:
Your sons will prophesy,
   also your daughters;
Your young men will see visions,
   your old men dream dreams.
When the time comes,
   I'll pour out my Spirit
On those who serve me, men and women both,
   and they'll prophesy.
I'll set wonders in the sky above
   and signs on the earth below,
Blood and fire and billowing smoke,
   the sun turning black and the moon blood-red,
Before the Day of the Lord arrives,
   the Day tremendous and marvelous;
And whoever calls out for help
   to me, God, will be saved.'"[4]

Peter described a spiritual movement caused by the explosive, visible, and world-altering power of the Holy Spirit invading the souls of men to advance the Kingdom of God. *This* is the endgame of the Holy Spirit and the moment we have been building to in our journey together in *Overflow*. The message from Peter then, and from me now, is that the Holy Spirit has designs on your moment in time, in your personal context, for your zones of influence, and he wants to work through you in meaningful ways in the rhythms of your everyday life. Where you live. Where you work. Where you pray. Where you play.

God wants *you* to be felt in your context.

At Pentecost, the most meaningful thing that could happen

in *that context* at that moment in time was for men to speak in discernible languages, praising God in ways that stunned people visiting from all over the world.

> There were many Jews staying in Jerusalem just then, devout pilgrims from all over the world. When they heard the sound, they came on the run. Then when they heard, one after another, their own mother tongues being spoken, they were blown away. They couldn't for the life of them figure out what was going on, and kept saying, "Aren't these all Galileans?"[5]

Purest shock. Strongest awe. Seen and felt impact after release.

Ask yourself: *What work of the Holy Spirit in me would be different or unusual for others to experience, help others to see God, and foster a sense of wonder over the power responsible for this activity?*

Our times are unprecedented in modern history. Much like in the time of our brother disciples of the first century, the global community is being turned upside down by events out of our control. Pandemics. Civil unrest. Fragile economies. Natural disasters. Rogue terrorism. Ethnic tensions. Encroaching government. Uncertain liberty. Redefined moral boundaries. Digital takeovers. Ubiquitous anxiety. The ground beneath the world's feet is sandy and tenuous. Personal dreams are being ruptured. Expectations of the future are being altered. Reality is biting. And because of technology, all of this is being recorded and broadcast on social media, turning our worries into panic.

Just like the first followers of Christ, even God's best are disillusioned, staring at the sky, waiting for the life they want and expected to appear. And while I am no angel dressed in white, I am your prophet on the page, and I am here to say to all men who speak Jesus' name worldwide: *"God's men! Why are you standing there looking into the sky? Leave yesterday behind. Jesus is coming back! It is not a time for standing still. It is a time to go into prayer with your brothers, to wait eagerly and expectantly, to get soaked in the Holy Spirit, and to release the power in you to a waiting and watching world!"*

Just as the world was ripe in the first century for an explosion of power through men equipped by the Holy Spirit, the global dynamics of change and challenge are laying the groundwork for a supernatural Kingdom harvest not seen since the day of Pentecost. Now, as then, a violent wind is rushing, and fire is falling on God's people—on those actively waiting for the ignition of the Holy Spirit. Now, as then, Spirit-empowered male culture will step into its Kingdom moment, spawning organic secondary movements of worship, spontaneous outreach, local justice, family and community renewal, and grassroots missions that will span the world and break generational dysfunctions. Now, as then, the Holy Spirit seeks to set you loose in *your* known world.

Where you live. Where you work. Where you pray. Where you play.

Time to Overflow and Spread

The image was a familiar one—water. Baptism to a first-century Jewish believer meant *getting soaked*. A complete and total covering of water physically represented a spiritual oneness with whatever message called for the baptism. John the Baptist's message was repentance, so getting baptized by him meant you intended to change your ways. So when Jesus said that John the Baptist's *outer* baptism would be matched by an *inner* baptism by the Holy Spirit and fire, the men of Galilee knew a couple of things. First, this was different. A fuller and deeper identification with Jesus and his message was on the horizon. Second, the powerful inner work would be followed by an equally powerful overflow of the Holy Spirit, spreading like fire released into a fertile environment.

As we learned in Parts I and II, the same thing is happening to us right now through the transforming work of the Holy Spirit as we "grow up in all aspects into [Christ]"[6]—inwardly in character and outwardly in conduct. The Holy Spirit has an audience waiting for that *outbound* eruption right now.

God says: "Somebody is waiting on you."

The baptism and fullness of the Spirit *in your life* is intended to produce a witness *in your known world*—your *overflow*. We are going to dive into the practical expressions of what that means in these final chapters. The book of Acts is still being written, and you're part of it because the Holy Spirit has not changed how he moves upon and through followers of Jesus. All the gifts of the Holy Spirit are still available for him to distribute to whomever he chooses, whenever he wants, and wherever on the planet he desires, just as he did with the first disciples *in their context*. He unilaterally decides who gets what gifts for his purposes. Advancing God's purposes in the spaces and places we find ourselves should be our pursuit.

> God's various gifts are handed out everywhere; but they all originate in God's Spirit. God's various ministries are carried out everywhere; but they all originate in God's Spirit. God's various expressions of power are in action everywhere; but God himself is behind it all. Each person is given something to do that shows who God is: Everyone gets in on it, everyone benefits. All kinds of things are handed out by the Spirit, and to all kinds of people! The variety is wonderful:

- wise counsel
- clear understanding
- simple trust
- healing the sick
- miraculous acts
- proclamation
- distinguishing between spirits
- tongues
- interpretation of tongues.

All these gifts have a common origin, but are handed out one by one by the one Spirit of God. He decides who gets what, and when.[7]

The book of Acts is a highlight reel of activating moments when men became dangerously effective agents of God's power, using the gifts he gave them. In the days to come, we will follow in their footsteps:

- Breaking cultural rules and touching the "untouchable"
- Praying with spiritual authority to turn the tide and bring healing and freedom
- Pressing the fight and accepting the cost of being salt, light, and an aroma of Christ
- Staying faithful in spite of heavy cultural opposition that wants to stop the Kingdom's advance
- Leading by serving in the local church
- Teaching, activating, encouraging, and equipping followers
- Identifying needs and volunteering to care for the needs of the least, the lost, and the left out
- Raising up other men "known to be full of the Spirit and wisdom"[8] and entrusting them with outreaches and missions

Now, as then, any of these exploits may follow a season of disillusionment, discouragement, and defeat. That's intentional and may be ordained by God so that his glory might shine all the brighter in your life. Now, as then, the Holy Spirit will come upon you (if he hasn't already), baptize you, fill you with a new insight into people, and beautifully unleash you to set your world on fire with the presence of God.

It will be the sound heard round the spiritual world.

Are you ready?

Holy Spirit,

Thank you for coming to me, dwelling in me, and filling up my life with new gifts and new purpose to replace old ways and old habits that didn't glorify you.

I want you to baptize my hopes and dreams afresh with your power. I want to overflow and spread your message about Jesus in the world around me. I want a blast zone of impact that causes others to wonder why a person like me is doing the things I am doing. I want to be salt, light, and an aroma of eternal life where I live, work, pray, and play. Every space is yours. Every place I go is yours. Every encounter I make is yours. Give me your eyes so I can see all the opportunities before me, big and small. This prayer is my flashpoint, my moment of decision—I yield to your work in me and through me.

Holy Spirit, you have my permission to use me in new ways. Enable me now. I am knocking and want you to swing the doors wide open. In Jesus' name I pray. Amen.

8

RELEASE CAPTIVES

I Am a Freedom Fighter

EVERY MAN HAS HIS "EGYPTS." Spiritually speaking, "Eygpts" represent those times, seasons, places, circumstances, experiences, and sets of people that call up strong feelings of powerlessness. They are low points on your life map. The promise offered by your Egypt may have appeared fun at the start or even seemed like a purpose for your life, but over time, it steadily becomes a place of enslavement, sickness, and self-destruction. In a broken world full of broken people trying to survive, no one makes it through this life unscathed by losses or setbacks.

In my own family, and as a mental-health worker and pastor, I have seen my share of enslaving circumstances:

- A season of debilitating depression or anxiety someone couldn't escape

- The chasing of the elusive "more" that only leaves a person poorer and lonelier
- Toxic family or other relationships
- The torture that comes from living a double life
- An unwitting drift into addiction
- Diving into unhealthy lifestyles as a solution to other problems
- Pursuing self-importance as a solution to a low self-perception
- Publicly projecting faith but privately being dominated by sin
- Becoming ensnared and controlled by a narcissistic spouse, boss, or church leader—all the while consumed with self-blame
- Living without God and in darkness spiritually

Egypts disable your spirit and mess with your self-perception. The dominant feeling is isolation. Your conscience tells you this is not your best life or the best version of yourself, but you have built an image or a lifestyle around your Egypt. You may have even invested significant relational capital. All that makes walking away from your personal Egypt a difficult prospect. From this place of inner conflict, you subconsciously envy other people's lives. *If only that were me*, you tell yourself. You analyze others' appearances, social media posts, and activities, comparing their projected outside image with your private inside reality. Upon comparison, per usual, you feel you are the only one who lives this way, with no rescue or deliverance in sight. Of course, you would be wrong, but that is what you believe, and your behavior flows out of your belief.

Streaming into this condition comes God and his good intentions for us in the midst of our spiritual, emotional, and psychological predicaments. God wants all people to experience freedom from captivities created by the devil—the pharaoh we unwittingly serve in our Egypts. Spinning lies for truth, the devil wants your life under his thumb—in ignorance, fear, or pride—offering powerful excuses that prevent spiritual escape.

Then and now, to the pharaoh of this world, God says, "Enough!"

Moses said to the people, "Always remember this day.
This is the day when you came out of Egypt from a house
of slavery. GOD brought you out of here with a powerful
hand."[1]

God rescued us from dead-end alleys and dark dungeons.
He's set us up in the kingdom of the Son he loves so
much, the Son who got us out of the pit we were in, got
rid of the sins we were doomed to keep repeating.[2]

That's what God does: he rescues everyone—me, you, anyone around you.

When God rescued me, the Holy Spirit flooded into every crevice of my heart and spirit, changing the way I saw life and even how I saw myself. Living water ran through my mind and life at five million cubic feet per second. My deliverance was like blowing the lid off a volcano, and it was all I could do to contain so much purpose, wisdom, security, identity, family, vision, forgiveness, acceptance, love, affirmation, and newfound freedom without weeping or witnessing or both!

The details of your story of deliverance from your personal Egypt may differ, but all followers of Jesus share a common story of deliverance from spiritual darkness and sin into the light of Christ, the Kingdom of God, and life in the Spirit. Whatever our spiritual backgrounds may be, this is the silver thread that connects us all against the dark backdrop of Adam's sin, which infected all Creation. Every pain man has ever experienced, every malady of evil that has ever touched him has its roots in Adam.

This first "Egypt" was not located along the Nile River—it was created willfully and spiritually in the garden of Eden. This place of oppression and isolation from God came into existence when man believed the lie that he could determine good and evil for himself instead of letting God define it. That belief led to a behavior that brought man into slavery without the power to remedy or reverse his situation.

The second "Egypt"—the literal, historical Egypt—and all other symbolic "Egypts" since, include one common denominator for God's people—a condition of captivity that brings pain to self and others. So when I say every man has his Egypt, a believer reflects on his *former identity*—living in the spiritual Egypt of the *former world* apart from Christ, held down by his *former partnership* with the culture, the sin nature within, and the devil.

A nonbeliever, whether knowingly or unknowingly, is still in spiritual Egypt, unable to experience God's love and purpose. The pharaoh of this world and his axis of evil still hold billions hostage, and he wants to keep them there. He is also intentionally chasing believers down by the millions, attempting to lure the delivered back to Egypt by playing upon their insecurities and discontent.

This is the real fight, the real *ongoing* story, where the real work of the Holy Spirit in and *through* us manifests in powerful ways.

> It wasn't so long ago that we ourselves were stupid and stubborn, easy marks for sin, ordered every which way by our glands, going around with a chip on our shoulder, hated and hating back. But when God, our kind and loving Savior God, stepped in, he saved us from all that. It was all his doing; we had nothing to do with it.[3]

It is called your *deliverance*.

His Fight for You Is Your Fight for Others

The fight for your *deliverance* is the work of the Holy Spirit.

God's initial spiritual work of deliverance in our lives, like Israel's literal deliverance, is *the first in a series of shaping encounters* that change how we relate to God. More specifically, as we'll see, it is the basis of the Spirit-formed, Spirit-filled, and Spirit-used life. Of little consequence to God is *the particulars* of your personal encounters with him. Of *massive* importance to God is your response to these experiences with him that *set you free*, how those deliverances shape your identity in him, and how the Holy Spirit seeks to use a delivered and Spirit-empowered man in the lives of others.

Moving God's people forward in God's purposes to advance God's Kingdom has always been God's intention. As a pastor, I am always seeking the best ways to get people off their "blessed assurance" and into their Spirit-appointed missions on earth. God's pioneering pastor, however, was Moses, who had to spiritually recalibrate his troops early and often after the greatest deliverance in human history up to that point. In fact, when he needed to light a fire beneath the feet of God's children, he had a tried-and-true formula to motivate, remind, and teach his people about their purpose on earth. It was undeniably the strongest possible reminder of the character of their God and his love for them—a simple way to think about their purpose as God's chosen representatives.

> For the LORD your God is God of gods and Lord of
> lords, the great God, mighty and awesome, who shows
> no partiality and accepts no bribes. He defends the cause
> of the fatherless and the widow, and loves the foreigner
> residing among you, giving them food and clothing.
> And you are to love those who are foreigners, for you

yourselves were foreigners in Egypt. Fear the LORD your
God and serve him. Hold fast to him and take your oaths
in his name. He is the one you praise; he is your God,
who performed for you those great and awesome wonders
you saw with your own eyes.[4]

As we seek to set the Holy Spirit's power loose in our unique
environments, we must consider the nature of God's intervention
in our lives. What he models in the act of delivering us is a lesson
for us to learn and, in turn, to live out.

A strong and tender God who delivers me

You yourselves were foreigners in Egypt.
DEUTERONOMY 10:19, NIV

Captives know what it feels like to be held against their will by
someone or some circumstance out of their control. God's Word
identifies humanity by nature as an "enslaved" population, held
hostage by sin, isolated from God, and consigned to spend eternity
away from his presence. But then God delivered us out of this
spiritual Egypt, not stopping with this one act but proceeding to
deliver us from ourselves progressively to this day. We are delivered
from unhealthy ways of thinking about ourselves and others. We
are delivered from expressions of fear and self-protection as God's
love penetrates and secures us emotionally. We are progressively
delivered from the clutches of out-of-control appetites and into a
life of freedom and self-discipline.

The Holy Spirit has authored not only our salvation but also
every transformation of character and conduct. He defends our
dignity. He provides hope. He fills us with faith. He secures our
peace. He restores our worth.

A strong and tender God who fights for your freedom

> The LORD your God is God of gods and Lord of lords,
> the great God, mighty and awesome, who shows no
> partiality and accepts no bribes.
> DEUTERONOMY 10:17, NIV

The Holy Spirit wants us always to have a right view of God because without one, our accountability to God and confidence in our mission are shot. He is unequaled, unparalleled, and unimpeachable in both strength and integrity. We have been delivered by and brought into relationship with a mighty and awesome God who fights to set his people free. He is our warrior-champion marching forth to battle for us. This liberating use of his strength for the sake of people he created in his image is the "family resemblance" the Holy Spirit is tasked with reproducing in believing sons.

A strong and tender God who defends the vulnerable

> He defends the cause of the fatherless and the widow, and
> loves the foreigner residing among you, giving them food
> and clothing.
> DEUTERONOMY 10:18, NIV

The Holy Spirit also wants us to reflect God's justice by defending the vulnerable—those held captive by their circumstances—who need a champion. Throughout Scripture, we repeatedly see God's heart for the marginalized, traumatized, neglected, lonely, abused, and exploited. The common denominator is that these captives are disconnected from the system. This affords God's people a meaningful context to impartially and energetically change the circumstances of those in need.

A strong and tender God who wants me to reflect his character in my conduct

> Fear the LORD your God and serve him. Hold fast to him and take your oaths in his name. He is the one you praise; he is your God, who performed for you those great and awesome wonders you saw with your own eyes.
>
> **DEUTERONOMY 10:20-21, NIV**

God's man shares God's heart. Making commitments "in his name" is synonymous with faithfully acting according to his character. His character defends the vulnerable, the captive, the marginalized, the persecuted, the oppressed, the lonely, the left out, and the left behind. If we are listening to the Holy Spirit, our hands and feet will take us toward the "foreigners" among us. People who are outside the borders of God's family but inside our contexts at any given moment—these are the ones God wants us to connect with and adopt into our circles of care and concern. It may take some time, some maturing, and some internal change first, but eventually, the Holy Spirit will raise up a tender warrior who is unafraid to stand up for those who need a spiritual champion to fight for them.

The Heart of the Gospel

The heart of God is at the heart of the gospel.

This desire to set the Holy Spirit loose in your corner of the world has a strong foundation connected with and rooted in the heart of the Father and is clearly expressed in the Son. To understand your relationship and responsibility to the Holy Spirit in your world, you must first clearly see how your story of deliverance(s) as a believer is an expression of the heart of God.

His movement toward you and for you is the exact picture your movement toward others should reflect. When we see our own deliverance clearly, we:

- See God more clearly
- Perceive our own condition and character more accurately
- Grasp Christ's mission on earth more meaningfully
- Understand the work of the Holy Spirit through us more fully
- Realize the goals of our ministry more fruitfully
- Identify with those we are called to reach more readily
- Identify with Christ as a tender warrior more visibly

Our basis is the Holy Spirit on, the Holy Spirit in, and the Holy Spirit working through Jesus to release captives.

"The Spirit of the Lord is on me, because he has anointed me to proclaim good news to the poor. He has sent me to proclaim freedom for the prisoners and recovery of sight for the blind, to set the oppressed free, to proclaim the year of the Lord's favor."
Then he rolled up the scroll, gave it back to the attendant and sat down. The eyes of everyone on the synagogue were fastened on him. He began by saying to them, "Today, this scripture is fulfilled in your hearing."[5]

Poor. Captive. Blind. Oppressed. Egypt.

These categories depict the *spiritual conditions* of the human spirit as well as the tangible condition of the people Jesus sought to engage, deliver, and set free spiritually, physically, and emotionally. Poor, captive, blind, and oppressed are conditions of soul, frames of mind, levels of insight, and degrees of bondage the Holy Spirit has been commissioned to fight against in order to bring liberty physically, emotionally, and spiritually. All require deliverance from Egypt and the pharaoh of the world. More practically, they define and describe *our* target audiences that the Holy Spirit will reveal to us for engagement.

All races. All ages. All environments. All people.

Where Christ's strong and tender warriors are deployed, the poor of spirit become wealthy. The starving are fed and become full. The lonely are comforted and included. Those who have no perception of God see him clearly. Wherever you are, the Holy Spirit is. And wherever the Holy Spirit is, there is a mission to set people free.

> Now the Lord is the Spirit, and where the Spirit of the Lord is, there is freedom. And we all, who with unveiled faces contemplate the Lord's glory, are being transformed into his image with ever-increasing glory, which comes from the Lord, who is the Spirit.[6]

The Holy Spirit transforms men to be like Jesus: fearless, focused, and filled with God's power to deliver freedom to waiting souls. In Acts 2:1-41, the Holy Spirit takes up this mission, raising up warriors to do his will. These Spirit-empowered men show us exactly how to express God's heart for spiritual captives. In these last chapters, we are going to see how the Holy Spirit wants to work through us to:

- Relieve someone's pain
- Reduce someone's load
- Raise someone's spirit
- Reach someone's soul

Jesus said we would be his witnesses—men who *give evidence* after seeing, experiencing, and encountering the Holy Spirit's *delivering power.*

Bring freedom!

Holy Spirit,

Thank you for seeking me out and setting me free. I remember my deliverance. I remember my Egypts and the condition of my heart and soul without God. I remember the joy of my salvation and your healing power in me over the years, changing me and giving me victory over my darkest sides. I reflect on the ongoing war within me and around me for freedom, and I need your power in my life for those fights. I need your continued work of release and healing in my life. I praise you for being my strong and mighty Deliverer.

Holy Spirit, I recognize your desire to deliver and set people free using me as your vessel. I accept. I want to be strong and tender like God, with a heart for captives suffering in bondage and blindness. As Jesus fought for my spiritual freedom, I accept the mission of fighting for others' freedom with your presence assuring me and anointing me for the work. Give me your eyes for the foreigner, the poor, the blind, the captive, and the oppressed. As I see, help me to pray. As I pray, make me willing to speak up, lift up, show up, and stand up for the ones Jesus loves and died for. Help me to forget myself and my needs so that I can enter their lives and respond to their need to know their Deliverer and experience new freedom. I'm running to the battle. In Jesus' name I pray. Amen.

9

RELIEVE SOMEONE'S PAIN

I Am a Comfort Bringer

IT WAS AN ANNUAL TRADITION for our family, one I looked forward to the whole year long. So in late November, I sent a text to a friend:

> *Hey Elizabeth . . . my family is praying for a single mother with children we can come alongside at Christmas. Do any of your people know of someone who is struggling to make ends meet as a single mom this Christmas?*

Her reply: *I know just the person.*

One month later, my son and I were at a massive apartment complex in town. It was a rainy December night and unusually cold for Southern California. Our car was loaded down with colorful bags of wrapped presents, and there was something joyful *and* risky about what we were doing. We joked that we were on a "mission from God" to find our "drop zone," deliver the "package," and rendezvous at "extraction point Charlie."

As we rolled down another street, I stared up through the windshield, squinting for clear lines of sight between the alternating blurry then clear strokes of the wipers, looking for a number.

I mumbled to myself and God at the same time: "Come on, 86. Where are you, baby? I need building number 86. Lord, show me building 86."

We had found the thirties and fifties section of the complex but were completely clueless about the housing numbers. Sensing another dead end, I put our truck in reverse *again*, mumbled some more, and turned down a different street hoping to encounter some divine providence.

On the new street, the numbers on the building to the right read *80*, then *82*, and so on until I pulled in front of unit *86*. Alleluia! The answer to prayer felt a bit like dumb luck, but I was overjoyed and relieved.

Me *(to my son)*: *Okay, dude. You are going to bring all this stuff to the door.*

Ryan: *Me? Why me?*

Me: *Because she might recognize me. But she has no clue who you are, and it's better that way. Apartment number 25 is right through this courtyard. You can see it from here. Look.*

I don't think Ryan would have hesitated had it not been for a shady-looking character having a smoke in the rain outside the building. Funny how a guy simply smoking can look menacing on a rainy night. He was positioned at the mouth of the courtyard too, appearing like a sentry. Ryan would have to walk by him to get to the apartment door, which I could see through the gap in the building.

Me: *I am right here watching you all the way. You have to do it. We don't have her phone number, and we can't leave the stuff on the porch in the rain. Besides, we have this guy right here hovering and watching us, so we definitely can't ring the doorbell and run. Look, I can see you the whole way. I am right here.*

Ryan: *Okay. What do I say?*

I bit my lip for a few seconds, staring out the window at the door with a gold-plated *25* on it, thinking about his question. With the truck engine running, the sound of rain peppering the roof, and a man taking another drag off his cigarette in the courtyard entrance, our *quest* was at a turning point. Helping a thirteen-year-old talk to an adult to deliver a bunch of gifts *anonymously*—courteously and nonthreateningly—is not as easy as it seems.

Me: *Okay, say this: "Are you Terrie?" So you can confirm we have the right place. Then say: "I have some gifts for you and your daughter." Then hand her the gifts and say, "Merry Christmas." That's all you need to do. Got it?*

Ryan nodded, got out of the truck, grabbed all the bags from the back seat, and was off to apartment number 25. He passed the cigarette man just fine, ambled through the rain across the courtyard, got to the green door, knocked on it, and waited.

After about thirty seconds, I had a sinking feeling that no one would answer. Our intel had said this was the best time to deliver.

I watched Ryan knock again and, after about five seconds, the door opened.

As Ryan quizzed the short Asian woman in the doorway, she looked a little perplexed. Her nod confirmed we had the right "contact" for delivery. Then I saw the woman look down quickly at her left leg where a three-year-old in footed pajamas clung to her pants, undoubtedly curious about the large boy holding packages.

Unable to hear any dialogue, I then saw Terrie shrug her shoulders, clasp her hands together over her chest, and engulf my son in what I know for him was an uncomfortably long bear hug. That's when, for me, time slowed and the moment hung in the air. For me as a dad, the image of my son and this single mom on that porch in the rain was one for the ages. I got to savor it for all of four seconds before Ryan was released from the grip of gratitude.

He gave his parting wish of "Merry Christmas" and then ran to the "extraction point." Jumping back into the truck, he was all smiles, his face flushed red and his breath visible from the cold.

Me: *So, how did it go?*

Ryan: *I told her I was just the delivery person and that the gifts were from a family at church. Then she hugged me.*

Me: *I saw that. Perfect. Great job. Let's roll.*

Mission accomplished.

For the entire year leading up to this cold December night, each member of the family had saved pennies, nickels, dimes, and quarters for the purpose of helping someone we would never know. No one talked about it. The days passed by. Leftover change hit jelly jars, mugs, jewelry boxes, and ashtrays in the family cars, accumulating steadily over the year. A few days before delivery day, the family spent an afternoon consolidating all the change—separating, counting, and making rolls of quarters, dimes, nickels, and pennies. This year, like every year, we had a contest to see who could guess the total amount saved as we looked forward to the final number we could put toward a family. We thought through the practical and personal needs of a single mom and plotted an attack plan for hitting different stores, getting gift cards, and selecting presents. We shopped, wrapped, prayed, and delivered. We owned this uniquely, start to finish.

The joy my family experienced comes from knowing that whoever God selects for us to serve is probably someone who feels alone in her circumstance, someone we can come alongside in Jesus' name. My family didn't know the emotional or psychological challenges of living as a single working mother. But that night we rejoiced that she was comforted and encouraged by God.

The hug my son received was worship. The smile on his face was worship. The joy I experienced on Christmas morning, as I imagined this little family opening our gifts, was worship. The renewed hope I discerned in Terrie's expression was worship. Why worship? Because when God meets us or someone else tangibly, the experience brings with it security, freedom, and encouragement to face the realities of life. It is a *theophany*—a visible manifestation to a human being that the God of the universe cares, has moved visibly toward that person, and is blessing him or her in real time and space.

When I think of Terrie the single mom and her authentic response to *Operation Solo Mama*, my mind goes to another woman, another theophany, and another occasion when a woman worshiped because God was thinking specifically about her and blessed her.

And Mary said, "I'm bursting with God-news; I'm
dancing the song of my Savior God. God took one good
look at me, and look what happened—I'm the most

fortunate woman on earth! What God has done for me will never be forgotten, the God whose very name is holy, set apart from all others."[1]

God is mindful of all who feel isolated and alone because of private issues they never anticipated or wanted. Are we? The Mighty One empowers his spiritually mighty followers to be mindful of those who suffer in silence in order to relieve the pain of loneliness and scarcity and create anthems of praise on earth. The Holy Spirit is calling us to enter and relieve pain around us, wherever and whenever possible.

> *While women weep, as they do now, I'll fight; while children go hungry, as they do now, I'll fight; while men go to prison, in and out, in and out, as they do now, I'll fight; while there is a poor lost girl upon the streets, while there remains one dark soul without the light of God, I'll fight, I'll fight to the very end!*[2]
>
> WILLIAM BOOTH

The Helper and His Helpers

The Holy Spirit in a man *brings help* to others through that man.

Jesus used the word *helper* four times in one discussion with his disciples to describe the nature and work of the Holy Spirit.[3] The Greek word is *paracletos*, and at its root are the concepts of advising, exhorting, comforting, strengthening, intervening, and encouraging.

When Jesus spoke to his men about the Helper, he knew the disciples soon would meet with trials. In a vertical sense, they would need all the assistance that the Helper could offer to stay faithful and productive in the midst of the greatest changes and challenges of their lives. In a horizontal sense, after being filled with the Holy Spirit's mighty presence and power, they would become agents of that same help, comfort, and encouragement, bringing healing and hope to others. The disciples would accomplish this by *standing up*, *showing up*, *lifting up*, and *speaking up* in the lives of the people they would encounter.

The Holy Spirit in a man channels meaningful help through that man.

Our little family tradition at Christmas is a good reminder to me that while "big" opportunities to help others rarely come, the small ones surround me daily. In baseball, they call it winning by "small ball," which is the strategy of getting base hits to advance base runners to score runs rather than relying on hitting home runs. As we seek to witness, giving evidence of our relationship to Christ through the power of the Holy Spirit, let's look simply and closely at the character and conduct of Christ as well as at the men of Pentecost—the followers who were the first human beings filled and empowered by the Holy Spirit. Both provide solid models of the Holy Spirit being set loose in a personal and cultural context to advance God's Kingdom. Observing their examples, we can then aggressively cooperate with the Holy Spirit to consistently:

- *Stand up* for the weak
- *Show up* to help others
- *Lift up* our brothers and sisters
- *Speak up* for Christ among those he died to save

As a consequence of acting in faith in these ways, the Holy Spirit is going to change you in four powerful ways:

- You will become more secure in Christ.
- You will be more directly supported by Christ.

- You will be empowered with more boldness in your walk with Christ.
- You will sense an advancement of your witness for Christ.

The initiative of the Holy Spirit through a man always results in a transformation of that man. The Holy Spirit validates God's presence and purposes in our lives as we act in faith.

Let's look at how Jesus and his Spirit-empowered men personally brought relief into the lives of others through the power of the Holy Spirit.

relief (n.): the feeling of happiness that occurs when something unpleasant or distressing stops or does not happen; removal or lessening of something painful or troubling; something that interrupts in a welcome way[4]

Helping Others Feel Secure

Jesus loved the *ragamuffins*, people who—for sociocultural reasons—felt God was far from them.

The Holy Spirit moved upon Jesus regularly to *stand up* for the vulnerable, stigmatized, and isolated to show them they were accepted by God, secure in his presence, and worthy of salvation. The ethnically, morally, physically, and culturally unacceptable were all deemed acceptable by his acceptance and connection to them. For these segments of the population, the religious class was not easy to be around. Yet these same outsiders seemed comfortable around Jesus. Lepers, prostitutes, Samaritans, tax collectors, gluttons, children, women, the diseased, crippled, mentally unstable, and garden-variety sinners were at home with Jesus because of the Spirit of the Lord upon him. In fact, the religious leaders' knock on Jesus was that his standards were very *low* when it came to his associations and locations for ministry. But working seamlessly with the Holy Spirit, Jesus fully expressed the heart of God toward these "foreigners" in his own culture, challenging the disciples on many levels and, on more than one occasion, causing reactions among them in response to his behavior.

Father, Son, and Holy Spirit are drawn to the *lonely and oppressed* because their spirits are crushed, their dignity is robbed, and without God's intervention, they seem to be facing a bleak future. So God—in the flesh—makes it his mission to restore *all three* back to them by supplying his presence and help. While on earth, Jesus called these people poor in spirit; they needed a physician to restore spiritual wealth, spiritual health, and spiritual insight. Some of Jesus' richest encounters were with those who were poorest in spirit, flipping the religious culture of the day on its head. These people were authentic, they were honest, they were not self-centered, and above all, they were free from hubris and agenda. What did Jesus do exactly? He brought needed *relief*—that feeling of joy that comes when distressing and unpleasant feelings inside are stopped by an action someone takes for you.

The men of Pentecost followed his example in the Spirit. Fresh from the upper room, they, too, ran head-on into cultural and religious discrimination against certain widows who had fallen through cracks in the system. It could have easily been glossed over in the chaos of the moment or in the name of embedded culture, but the Holy Spirit would not allow it. Instead, men "full of the Holy Spirit" mobilized to bring relief and security to those who felt forgotten.

> During this time, as the disciples were increasing in
> numbers by leaps and bounds, hard feelings developed
> among the Greek-speaking believers—"Hellenists"—toward

the Hebrew-speaking believers because their widows were being discriminated against in the daily food lines. So the Twelve called a meeting of the disciples. They said, "It wouldn't be right for us to abandon our responsibilities for preaching and teaching the Word of God to help with the care of the poor. So, friends, choose seven men from among you whom everyone trusts, men full of the Holy Spirit and good sense, and we'll assign them this task. Meanwhile, we'll stick to our assigned tasks of prayer and speaking God's Word."

The congregation thought this was a great idea. They went ahead and chose—

Stephen, a man full of faith and the Holy Spirit,
Philip,
Procorus,
Nicanor,
Timon,
Parmenas,
Nicolas, a convert from Antioch.

Then they presented them to the apostles. Praying, the apostles laid on hands and commissioned them for their task.

The Word of God prospered. The number of disciples in Jerusalem increased dramatically. Not least, a great many priests submitted themselves to the faith.[5]

Widows—victims of discrimination—meet your new best friends: *men full of the Holy Spirit. Kaboom!* Cultural barriers crumbled, the vulnerable were not victimized, the onlookers were blown away, and hearts melted. The result? A fresh wave of

God-awareness took over the streets and synagogues, resulting in yet another explosion of growth in the believing community. All of this because people who *had been* left out were provided relief, intentionally included, and cared for in their desperation. The Holy Spirit in a community of God's men was saying: "Make them secure. Don't forget them because of racial or other issues. Give them your best men and best efforts, and watch what happens!"

The strong and clear message: *Include everybody! Exclude nobody.*

When you look at the ministry of Jesus and the believers at Pentecost, you see relief happening. It looked like centuries-old walls falling down: ethnic walls, cultural walls, economic walls, and even religious walls. You can't miss this! The Holy Spirit was at work transcending established culture to make the most vulnerable among them feel secure. In the process, everyone present witnessed the authority of the Kingdom of God over a culture that had left people out. A higher and better allegiance was seen; a witness started building; men stood up for the weak and the vulnerable; and crazy good stuff started happening. That is the story of the men of Pentecost.

This will be your story as well.

The Holy Spirit wants to demonstrate to the world that God's man operates under a higher purpose, a royal one that gives him freedom to cross all cultural lines to make sure people feel included or, better, to *feel worthy* of inclusion. Think about it. There have been times in your life when you were not included. Did you feel less worthy than others? It may have even seemed your soul was under attack. But when you were included when you didn't think you would be, your soul was lifted, wasn't it? Every Spirit-empowered man locks into his higher purpose, which allows him to enter freely into the lives of people without hesitation over their worthiness. Evil knows that when men act selfishly they will practice *selective sympathy*. The Holy Spirit says God does not play favorites—ever.

> You do well when you complete the Royal Rule of the Scriptures: "Love others as you love yourself." But if you play up to these so-called important people, you go against the Rule and stand convicted by it. You can't pick and choose in these things, specializing in keeping one or two things in God's law and ignoring others. The same God who said, "Don't commit adultery," also said, "Don't murder." If you don't commit adultery but go ahead and murder, do you think your non-adultery will cancel out your murder? No, you're a murderer, period.
>
> Talk and act like a person expecting to be judged by the Rule that sets us free. For if you refuse to act kindly, you can hardly expect to be treated kindly. Kind mercy wins over harsh judgment every time.[6]

The Holy Spirit does not single out some and leave out others.

All of us have felt rejected by others and have been lonely because of it at some point in our lives. The Holy Spirit hates that feeling as much as we do. The opportunity to go from a creation of God to a child of God is available to all. Then, if you are a member of God's family, know that there are no cousins or in-laws—only sons and daughters who reflect the Father, Son, and Spirit.

> *secure (adj.): free from danger; free from risk of loss; easy in mind; assured . . . having no doubt*[7]

The Holy Spirit says: "Provide my relief by making others feel secure."

A Spirit-empowered man helps others to feel secure through inclusion.

> And you also were included in Christ when you heard the message of truth, the gospel of your salvation. When you believed, you were marked in him with a seal, the promised Holy Spirit, who is a deposit guaranteeing our inheritance until the redemption of those who are God's possession—to the praise of his glory.
> **EPHESIANS 1:13-14, NIV**

There was a time when you and I were not first family. God *let you in.* The Holy Spirit signed for you and marked you for first-class delivery to heaven. You didn't earn it or deserve it. Such a man, accepted graciously by God, *should be* the most accepting and inclusive man on the planet. God wants us to remember that the Kingdom of God is open for business to *all* who come in contact with it. This is especially true for those who have been made to feel less than worthy or that they've been left out of God's plan in any way.

A Spirit-empowered man helps others to feel secure through protection.

> Pure and genuine religion in the sight of God the Father means caring for orphans and widows in their distress and refusing to let the world corrupt you.
> **JAMES 1:27, NLT**

You can act according to embedded cultural values or listen promptly to the Holy Spirit in the character of Christ. A tender warrior looks after those in his context who are vulnerable and unable to defend themselves. As a collective group worldwide, Spirit-empowered men are a sleeping giant who can, if united, turn the tide to end the world's worst exploitations of women and children and engage in the greatest expression of justice ever seen. This is Christ, this is the Spirit-filled man of Pentecost, and this is us! We *look after* the vulnerable ones to prove our faith and say no to the culture's exploitation, apathy, and neglect.

A Spirit-empowered man helps others to feel secure through provision.

> My dear children, let's not just talk about love; let's practice real love.
> **1 JOHN 3:18**

Sympathy *is not a substitute* action. Though we were "foreigners" to God, the Holy Spirit, moving in partnership with Jesus, loved sacrificially and heroically on our behalf in order to bring about our salvation and transformation. Jesus provided his body and blood to secure salvation for all who believe. The Holy Spirit will prompt you to sacrifice materially to help others know the peace and security of being provided for by God.

A Spirit-empowered man helps others to feel secure by providing direction.

> Jesus straightened up and asked her, "Woman, where are they? Has no one condemned you?"
> "No one, sir," she said.

> "Then neither do I condemn you," Jesus declared.
> "Go now and leave your life of sin."
>
> **JOHN 8:10-11**, NIV

Jesus directed the would-be judge and jury of the adulteress to take a long hard stare in the mirror, and in doing so, perhaps he helped her to feel safer. But he didn't stop there. He also directed the adulteress *away from* what created the most pain and insecurity—a life of sin. A solid and sure direction for life is a relief.

This is how Jesus operated, and this is where the Holy Spirit wants to advance the Kingdom of God through your faith in action. But first, we must heed Scripture's warning about selective sympathy, take a strong look in the mirror, and define what authentic faith in action looks like in the life of a man of God. Jesus and the men of Pentecost suggest that authentic faith means submission to a higher purpose—one that gives us freedom to enter into the lives of others who mistakenly believe they are far from God's care and concern.

Holy Spirit,

I accept your mission to the vulnerable ones in my world. Today, make me a champion of someone who is feeling isolated and forgotten because of their circumstances. Bring somebody to my mind right now or—even better—bring someone across my path that I can come alongside to be your strong hands and feet. Forgive me for merely being sympathetic toward the vulnerable and thinking that is adequate. Help me to give of myself in order to restore someone's dignity and worth in your name. That's what you did for me! Help me to remember that as I move about my day and encounter others. Give me the courage and freedom, Holy Spirit, to cross cultural lines that prevent your love from flowing to those in need. Thank you, Holy Spirit, for helping me to sense, in your love, your inclusion of me, your protection of me, your provision for me, and your direction to me. I am ready to help others experience this same love. Now, help me to be a reflection of you in the lives of others. In Jesus' name I ask all these things. Amen.

10

REDUCE SOMEONE'S LOAD

I Am a Burden Sharer

"DID MY CALF MUSCLES JUST SNAP?" It felt like somebody had hit me with a baseball bat on the back of my leg. I'd been backpedaling quickly on the football field, watching the developing play closely so I could make a break on the ball once it was thrown. When I saw the ball release and head in my direction, I immediately planted my right foot and tried to push off. That's when I heard an awful sound, felt excruciating pain in my calf, and crumpled to the ground. It looked grotesque, and I feared the worst—not so much the *physical* consequences of my latest sports injury but the *relational* consequences it would create with my wife.

Say what? It was the setup for a perfect husband–wife storm.

Back home, my family was in the middle of packing up our two-story home. We were moving in just six days, and my wife,

Chrissy, was hard at work to get everything ready. As I left to play that day, she lovingly fired a *warning* across the bow of my conscience: "If you get injured playing football, I am going to kill you." Her sixth sense had told her that with the move upon us, a potentially ruinous scenario might play out, i.e., *Kenny plays hard, and if he plays, there is a distinct possibility Kenny could be out of commission physically.* Now you know why the physical pain was secondary to the emotional firestorm waiting for me back at "Packing Central."

My wife's best and only mule was dead.

When it comes to marital stress, *moving* is right up there with money issues, job transfers, unwed teenage pregnancies, sexual dysfunction, the empty-nest syndrome, midlife crises, and menopause. Bad news like mine *during a move* magnifies that tension, especially when the moving company is *you.*

I can usually work around obstacles and come up with alternative solutions, but a ruptured tendon was like Alcatraz: *there is no escape from this island.* This time, I could forget about using my resourcefulness, intellect, or emotional fortitude, none of which can magically heal a tendon. This was made painfully clear the next day at the orthopedic office when the doctor told me I should have heeded Chrissy's warning.

Thanks a lot, Doc. And I am paying for this?

The next several days magnified my predicament as Chrissy and my mother-in-law feverishly wrapped, boxed, and organized our belongings for the move. I felt like they should put me in the giveaway pile. I wasn't just *feeling* useless to them; I *was* useless.

After five days of trying to hop around, it was clear that I was not going to be able to carry anything. I needed help, but it was Friday, and we were moving the next day. Who would be able to come with such short notice? That's when my cell phone rang.

Darren: *Kenny, it's Darren. How're you doing?*

Me: *Not so hot, dude.*

Darren *(reacting to my man pain)*: *I don't know if I can come, but I'll see what I can do.*

Me: *Thanks, Darren.*

At 8 a.m. the next morning, I heard the rumbling of a large truck growling loudly down our street. Limping from the house to the driveway, I made it out in time to see a huge flatbed construction truck with removable sides pull up to my house. In the back were twenty guys Darren had rallied to the cause. These men looked like a platoon of fresh Marines ready for war. They jumped right out, filed into my home, and started hauling tables, mattresses, the washing machine—all the heavy stuff—out to the truck. Smiling behind the wheel of the big truck was Darren, the patron saint of desperate masculinity.

I wanted to leap for joy, but a firm handshake and "Thaaaaaank you" would have to do. My heart leaped on the inside.

Chrissy's face was transfixed by the sight of all this *energy* going to work for her and bailing me out.

I have never been so helpless, so happy, and so unburdened in the same moment. *My load* was being carried.

All these guys abandoned their Saturday plans when Darren put out the call. They brought themselves, their tools, and their big hearts to help me move and resettle. They did in six hours what would have taken my wife and a few others two whole days. They installed the washer and dryer, put beds together, placed all the furniture exactly where Chrissy wanted it, and did *all of the heavy lifting*. The Seventh Cavalry on horseback, Patton's

Third Army on the march, the Eighty-Second Airborne parachuting in, and the Spanish Armada in formation on the high seas couldn't have looked more glorious to me than that flatbed full of Spirit-empowered men rolling up to my driveway that Saturday morning.

These men went the second mile for me.

Make Lighter

When Jesus was explaining to his disciples how they would *really* turn heads, he gave them a picture that did not compute. He engaged in what could best be described as rhetorical overstatement to make his followers look closely at their own values. It was a *deliberate and obvious* exaggeration designed intentionally to challenge his followers, address an issue, and make a point.

> You have heard that it was said, "Eye for eye, and tooth for tooth." But I tell you, do not resist an evil person. If anyone slaps you on the right cheek, turn to them the other cheek also. And if anyone wants to sue you and take your shirt, hand over your coat as well. If anyone forces you to go one mile, go with them two miles. Give to the one who asks you, and do not turn away from the one who wants to borrow from you.[1]

Say what?

If Jesus' followers took what Jesus said literally, they were about to spend their entire lives being abused, codependent, naked, and broke! Jesus' words were clearly intended to strike at an issue central to his own life mission, the people he would die for, and the ongoing work of the Holy Spirit through his disciples. He used the same type of hyperbole another time. To get people to take sin seriously, he told them to gouge out their eyeballs and cut off their hands.[2] So what was the issue his followers needed to take seriously here?

Human selfishness, or "getting yours."

Jesus' point in this uncomfortable but forceful exposé on human selfishness is this: As a follower, you should seek opportunities to rein in your rights, be unusually selfless, and leave the perceived injustices that befall you with God. All these actions are counterintuitive to human nature, and they have the power to prompt curiosity. They demonstrate to others that you are under the control of something—or Someone! They communicate to those around you that natural human reactions like self-protection and stinginess are not the norm for you. And most convincingly, to be at peace in taking this action—even joyful—is a telltale sign of the presence of the Holy Spirit. The person experiencing your actions might think, *Well, this is a bit unusual.*

Exactly. Higher forces are at work. They are witnessing the *super*natural.

The whole second-mile reference may have been a lightning rod for any first-century Jewish citizen. At the time, Palestine was occupied by the Roman army, and because the government didn't pay for all of a soldier's provisions, the occupying soldiers could requisition whatever they needed from the conquered people. Roman soldiers were known to abuse the privilege, so this issue was likely a hot button for all Jews living under Roman rule. When asked, the residents of Israel might have had to stop what they were doing and carry a soldier's armor or pack for *one mile*. For every Jew listening to Jesus, going a *second* mile to serve the oppressor and occupier was unthinkable.

And that is exactly what Jesus knew they would be thinking, so it provided a perfect backdrop to contrast what his own life of Kingdom service and Holy Spirit living was all about. Only shocking and sacrificial actions in the presence of injustice would advance the cause. Jesus was emphatic here: his followers could not move the Kingdom of God forward without paying a price and serving others *extravagantly* in counterintuitive ways. By doing the unexpected to make *someone else's* load lighter, Jesus' followers would capture others' attention, making them wonder at such action, thus creating an opportunity for an encounter with the Holy Spirit.

Jesus modeled this "shock service" to his men. He served *them* as they ate, washed *their* feet, cooked *them* breakfast, and ultimately, died for *them* on the cross. In the process, he didn't squash their desire for greatness; he simply redefined the meaning of *great*.

> They were bickering over who of them would end up the greatest. But Jesus intervened: "Kings like to throw their weight around and people in authority like to give themselves fancy titles. It's not going to be that way with you. Let the senior among you become like the junior; let the leader act the part of the servant.
>
> "Who would you rather be: the one who eats the dinner or the one who serves the dinner? You'd rather eat and be served, right? But I've taken my place among you as the one who serves."[3]

The Servant King? Exactly. Greatness serves.

For those witnessing the transformation of Jesus' first followers, the most meaningful and authentic acts they could observe took the form of an unprecedented tsunami of service and ministry to people. Not coincidentally, these *supernatural* actions through the *supernatural* force of the Holy Spirit generated *supernatural* results.

That day about three thousand took [Peter] at his word, were baptized and were signed up. They committed themselves to the teaching of the apostles, the life together, the common meal, and the prayers.

Everyone around was in awe—all those wonders and signs done through the apostles! And all the believers lived in a wonderful harmony, holding everything in common. They sold whatever they owned and pooled their resources so that each person's need was met.

They followed a daily discipline of worship in the Temple followed by meals at home, every meal a celebration, exuberant and joyful, as they praised God. People in general liked what they saw. Every day their number grew as God added those who were saved.[4]

Overflow.
Now, on the other side of Jesus' sacrifice and departure, filled with insight and Holy Spirit power, the men of Pentecost were on fire and ready to serve others in humility and selflessness in their personal context.

They were now carrying the load.

The Holy Spirit in the man of God wants to relieve people of their burdens.

Are you tired? Worn out? Burned out on religion? Come to me. Get away with me and you'll recover your life. I'll show you how to take a real rest. Walk with me and work with me—watch how I do it. Learn the unforced rhythms of grace. I won't lay anything heavy or ill-fitting on you. Keep company with me and you'll learn to live freely and lightly.[5]

The mission of the Holy Spirit *in you* is to make this unburdening by Jesus real in your experience with him. The mission of the Holy Spirit *through you* is to make God real to others by unburdening them in unexpected ways. This unburdening is unexpected because people are used to seeing and experiencing so much self-interest and self-absorption in their daily rhythms. They are used to people not seeing people as people! So when they encounter men filled with the Holy Spirit who are called to abandon agendas, rights, offended feelings, politics, and cultural bias—men who will drop everything to lighten their load—it is unusual.

This is Jesus. These are acts of the apostles. This is you.

Spirit-filled men end up doing things they never imagined to testify to Jesus' work in and through them. In fact, lightening the load of others is so mission critical that Coach Paul the apostle was told by the Holy Spirit to make it a command for every New Testament believer.

> Live creatively, friends. If someone falls into sin, forgivingly restore him, saving your critical comments for yourself. *You* might be needing forgiveness before the day's out. Stoop down and reach out to those who are oppressed. Share their burdens, and so complete Christ's law. If you think you are too good for that, you are badly deceived.[6]

The Holy Spirit will help you reduce someone's load in the following ways:

The Spirit-empowered man helps others to feel lighter through his presence.

> When we arrived in Macedonia province, we couldn't settle down. The fights in the church and the fears in

our hearts kept us on pins and needles. We couldn't relax because we didn't know how it would turn out. *Then the God who lifts up the downcast lifted our heads and our hearts with the arrival of Titus.*
2 CORINTHIANS 7:5-6, EMPHASIS MINE

When you think about the most meaningful way to release the power of the Holy Spirit in your community, remember this: *everyday life is heavy!* Your very presence in the midst of a season of pressure relieves and comforts people.

I love watching the supernatural be *super* natural through Titus. He shows up, and soon the others around him have gone from heavy and harassed to light and delighted. We carry each other's burdens by simply showing up to help. As we arrive and engage people, the pressure gets *redistributed* and sometimes even eliminated. The Holy Spirit may have brought others into your life right now who need your simple presence to help carry the load they are under. Surprise somebody, show up in their life, and ask this one question, which is loaded with Holy Spirit potential: "Do you need anything?"

Ask this question wherever you go. Ask it of whoever you are with. Ask it at home with family members. Ask it on the job with coworkers. Ask it with neighbors. Ask it with fellow believers. Ask it when you hear of a loss. Ask it in faith, believing that God has you there to help carry whatever burden, small or large, physical or emotional, material or spiritual, someone may have. Ask in faith, committing to serve and act.

Whoever wants to be great must become a servant.
Whoever wants to be first among you must be your slave.
That is what the Son of Man has done: He came to serve,

not be served—and then to give away his life in exchange for the many who are held hostage.[7]

The Spirit-empowered man helps others to feel lighter by providing what's missing.

> The whole congregation of believers was united as one—one heart, one mind! They didn't even claim ownership of their own possessions. No one said, "That's mine; you can't have it." They shared everything. The apostles gave powerful witness to the resurrection of the Master Jesus, and grace was on all of them.
>
> ACTS 4:32-33

The Holy Spirit has made significant Kingdom impact and overflow this simple—*fill the hole!* His best work through us is not fancy. When you see someone burdened by a particular need right in front of you and you have the ability to help meet that need *now*, simply ask: "What do you need?" Or simply respond. Opportunities—big and small—are all around you. You only have to turn your ears on.

For example, one day, when I overheard the huge audio-video guy in our church building was only going to have an orange for his lunch, the Holy Spirit said, "Kenny, go across the street, buy him a burrito, and fill his stomach." In my spirit, I saluted. With my body, I left the building, got a massive carne asada burrito, came back, and plopped the food sack in front of him.

He seemed aghast. "Is this for me?" he asked.

"You are not eating only an orange for lunch!" I replied.

That's the Holy Spirit filling a physical hole. Sometimes it may be an emotional or spiritual hole you fill.

Remember: life creates holes, and the presence of the Holy Spirit in you fills them.

The Spirit-empowered man helps others to feel lighter by praying God's Word over issues weighing them down.

God's Word is an *indispensable* weapon. In the same way, prayer is essential in this ongoing warfare. Pray hard and long. Pray for your brothers and sisters. Keep your eyes open. Keep each other's spirits up so that no one falls behind or drops out.

EPHESIANS 6:17-18

When you feel heavy, you want to stop trying. When you feel light, it motivates you to keep going. Think of God's Word as powerful ammunition and prayer as the delivery system that brings that power to bear on a specific target.

I may not be able to take on many of the burdens I come in contact with, but I know Someone who *can*. Coming alongside people with the power of God's person and promises through prayer outperforms and outstrips our abilities and resources.

Wherever you find yourself, know that the Holy Spirit is ready at any moment and in any space to take on *any need*. A Spirit-empowered man has no reason to hesitate in bringing God's power and peace into a heavy situation through prayer. In fact, the Holy Spirit wants it to be his lifestyle.

Needs around us quickly outstrip our ability to meet them—we are each just one person! But God's man takes those same needs to God. The result? Oftentimes, people will feel lighter as we ask God to share the load.

Don't fret or worry. Instead of worrying, pray. Let petitions and praises shape your worries into prayers, letting God know your concerns. Before you know it, a sense of God's wholeness, everything coming together for good, will come and settle you down. It's wonderful what happens when Christ displaces worry at the center of your life.[8]

Through prayer, the principle of displacement is at work. Panic and worry are displaced by prayer. Heaviness is replaced by lightness. Oppressive fear is ousted, and the power of faith is restored. Sadness is mitigated by the redeeming hope of God's love and his ability to use the worst things to bring about his good purposes. Your faith in God manifested through your declaration of the Word of God over others in prayer dislodges spiritual and emotional oppression.

Remember, you have strong weapons. They are meant to be *put to work* for others.

The Spirit-empowered man helps others to feel lighter by providing insight.

But when the Friend comes, the Spirit of the Truth, he will take you by the hand and guide you into all the truth there is.

JOHN 16:13

The Holy Spirit is the single greatest giver of counsel and advice in all time and eternity. Pause for a second and let that sink in. The reason for this is simple—he is God and delivers God's wisdom in real time and space for God's purposes. He says the truest things about everything! He can't stop being who he is and won't cease to imbue everything he touches with truth.

He is living in you.

When people are in the midst of heavy circumstances and feeling the pressure, their ability to think clearly is almost always clouded.

As a race, we human beings are emotionally driven. When triggered, powerful feelings sabotage common sense by moving us to believe and behave in ways that make no sense! We either think things are fatal and final, or we wrongly assume everything's going to be okay— because then we don't have to accept responsibility to deal with stuff in the moment. In both cases, what we need is someone who doesn't have an agenda or conflict of interest who can come alongside, assess the situation, and offer a solution. To this end, Jesus said people are like sheep, and sheep don't survive without receiving *a lot* of direction.

> The heartfelt counsel of a friend is as sweet as perfume
> and incense.[9]

Remember the whole thing about being an aroma for God? Your presence—or more accurately, the Holy Spirit's presence in you— has a strong and visceral power when people need clarity. Emotions can cloud wisdom. Circumstances and pressure can cloud a person's decision-making. But when you come along as a Spirit-empowered and Word-filled friend, the 800-pound-gorilla situation sitting on their chests turns back into a hamster-size problem. Sometimes, the insight makes the person feel sensational, and other times it demands obedience. In either case, their heavy load gets lighter because of godly insight.

That's why you are there!

> So now you can pick out what's true and fair,
>   find all the good trails!
> Lady Wisdom will be your close friend,
>   and Brother Knowledge your pleasant companion.
> Good Sense will scout ahead for danger,
>   Insight will keep an eye out for you.
> They'll keep you from making wrong turns,

or following the bad directions
Of those who are lost themselves
    and can't tell a trail from a tumbleweed,
These losers who make a game of evil
    and throw parties to celebrate perversity,
Traveling paths that go nowhere,
    wandering in a maze of detours and dead ends.[10]

All who wander don't have to stay lost. The Holy Spirit's insight, spoken through you, turns out to be very practical in nature and can create real solutions that honor God and others.

The simple reality is that when others receive insight to know what to do, it makes life lighter by bringing clarity and much-needed perspective.

Holy Spirit,

It feels amazing to know that my load of guilt and sin has been lifted and replaced with a feathery blanket of forgiveness and hope. There are no words that properly express my gratitude. Thank you for continuing to carry and lighten my burdens in my fight with sin, to ease my struggle to make sense of circumstances, and to reduce my anxieties over the future. In this moment, I accept the mission to bring the same relief to others. Help me to clearly see the border where my abilities end and yours begin. Help me to see the simple ways I can be used to alleviate the heavy loads people are carrying by providing what's missing, supplying insight, entering into opportunities to pray, or simply making myself available. Use me to do some heavy lifting, Lord. I am your servant. Help me to start lightening the load in my own first-mile responsibilities and then move me to the second mile for people I can help. I pray now for the burdened around me in Jesus' powerful name. Amen.

11

RAISE SOMEONE'S SPIRIT

I Am a Strengthener of Spirits

SOMETIMES THE MEDIA has a field day with how men relieve their stress. Ask the marketing team that came up with the *What Happens Here, Stays Here* Las Vegas ad campaign. Years later, it's still the model for how the world says to deal with the isolating pressures of life. The offer is direct: escape it, medicate it, or distract it with another feeling, and then go back again to business as usual. Press repeat as often as needed.

That's one way.

Or you can *distribute the pressure* by having strong relationships with God and others, *make use of the pressure* to grow in these relationships, and enjoy regret-free downtime. This model of dealing with the pressures keeps more money in your wallet, your wife and kids loving you, and your body and mind free of headaches, hangovers, or holdover memories that pollute your life with guilt.

The Holy Spirit has given us all the right tools to deal with pressure, and the spiritual armor necessary to defend against an enemy who relentlessly suggests that taking a walk on the wild side will not hurt anybody.[1] One of our most powerful weapons in this battle to reduce pressure, dampen the power of temptation, and produce spiritual endurance is something every man craves but gets very little of. We thirst for it the way a parched man on a hot Texas day needs cold water but subsists on his own saliva.

It's called *encouragement*.

I Never Knew

Me: *Pick you up in five minutes, and we'll go over to Cane's.*

Lance: *Okay, I'll be outside the building.*

During my time at Saddleback Church, before I joined the pastoral team at Crossline, my friend Lance and I would meet monthly as pastors in order to vent a little in a safe environment and check in with each other as brothers. I always looked forward to these times because, to me, Lance was like Yoda from Star Wars and I was like a young Padawan apprentice, gleaning in the fields of his experience and wisdom. His feedback and throwaway comments were so good that sometimes I left lunch with two pages of notes! He never had an agenda, and neither did I. We would just show up and start dialoguing over what projects we were working on, what messages we were preaching, family member updates, theology, and the future, all between bites of food and sips of iced tea.

It was on the tail end of one of these get-togethers that Lance unintentionally dropped a bomb on me. We were back in the church parking lot, sitting in my big Dodge, tying up our last topic of conversation. Lance was in the passenger seat, and as I told him that

I would follow up on some of the stuff we'd discussed, I expected him to say, "Great, Kenny. I'll talk to you soon" or "Cool, Kenny. Thanks for lunch" or "Next time, it will be my treat"—something that would put a period at the end of this long, run-on sentence we'd called lunch. Instead, Lance opted for a comma and released a cruise missile triangulated to hit me dead center in the heart:

"Kenny, I don't know if anybody has told you this lately, but I just want you to know how much we appreciate all you are doing here with the men of the church. I know how much energy and effort you are putting in, so I just wanted to tell you thanks for all you do."

KABOOM.

Suddenly I found my breathing interrupted and my eyes welling up. *What is happening to you, Kenny?* I thought. *C'mon, man, pull yourself together!* In a split second, however, I realized that my attempts to stop the flood of emotion rising within me were useless. Lance was witnessing my little meltdown from a distance of exactly one foot! Did he think I was going to confess a moral failure, adulterous affair, or grievous mistake that I couldn't hold in any longer? I couldn't look at him, which, I imagined, must have really made him think the worst. As I stared at the dashboard of my car, I could feel tears squeezing out of my eyes, rappelling down my face, and making a soft tapping noise on my pants. *What on earth is happening to you, Luck?*

Lance, thankfully, was completely silent and waited.

After wiping my nose with the back side of my hand, I grabbed my shirt and dabbed my eyes a few times. I took in a massive lungful of air, then exhaled through pursed lips, my cheeks bulging. It's that noisy blowing out a breath people do right before they confess or say something emotional. With my voice catching, I gave Lance my best interpretation of why his words had made me react this way:

"Wow, Lance. Sorry about this. I don't know exactly where this reaction is coming from, but I have a good idea. Your words caught me at a real interesting time. I have been asking myself lately if anyone really knows or cares about what I do. I have been at this church for fourteen years, so people assume I am doing fine. It appears I needed someone to say something like that to me today. I guess the combination of where I'm at and what you said hit a nerve. You really caught me off guard at a time when I was questioning if I should continue pressing the fight. I guess I was a little starved for some encouragement. The feedback from the guys is great, but this is different . . . as you can see, obviously. So thanks. Thanks a lot. It means a lot to me to know that."

The Holy Spirit was being the Holy Spirit through Lance just being Lance.

Sounds funny to say it that way, but it makes the most sense to me. God knew I needed some validating. He saw my passion ebbing, my endurance waning, and my confusion growing in the absence of some encouragement to keep fighting for the vision he had laid on my heart for men in my church and around the world. So the Lord sent me Lance, a Spirit-empowered man, as his messenger for the purpose of strengthening and steadying my feet in the midst of my doubts. Looking back, I remember that moment like it was yesterday, because it was so catalytic in my fight to stick with the vision of Every Man Ministries, the organization I founded to revolutionize men's ministry, free men spiritually, and ignite spiritual health worldwide. In many ways, I believe I am still here today, having been given the privilege of personally touching millions of men, in large part due to those two sentences uttered almost a decade ago.

High Demand, Low Supply

encourage (v.): to make more determined, hopeful, or confident; to spur on; to inspire with courage, spirit, or hope [2]

The Holy Spirit is a strong voice of encouragement in the family of God.

As we *push forward* to learn exactly what it looks like to set the Holy Spirit loose in our world, we must again look to the character and expressions of the Father, Son, and Holy Spirit in Scripture—as well as at the men of Pentecost—to get some insight into Spirit-empowered encouragement through God's man.

The Father encouraged the Son in his identity.

> The moment Jesus came up out of the baptismal waters, the skies opened up and he saw God's Spirit—it looked like a dove—descending and landing on him. And along with the Spirit, a voice: "This is my Son, chosen and marked by my love, delight of my life."
> **MATTHEW 3:16-17**

At this point in Jesus' earthly life, he had not preached one message. He had not performed one miracle or healed one person. There was no following. This blast of encouragement was the pure stuff—not based on what he did but on who he was.

No conditions. No reciprocity implied or required. There it is.

The timing was intentional as Jesus was about to begin an arduous and very public journey of revealing himself to the world. He would then be humiliated for it and would equip twelve men to carry a worldwide movement forward. It was important for the Father to let the Son know—at this precise moment—that he was loved and to give Jesus, in his humanity, the exact encouragement from divinity that every man needs and longs for. The Holy Spirit was active in this moment too, descending upon Jesus with encouragement and love, and turning both into powerful inner help.

How relevant this is to us as men, because when someone sees us, knows who we are at a personal level, and offers authentic encouragement, it strengthens us! Authentic encouragement happens in person, at the right time, and addresses the person rather than their performance or appearance. Your thoughts and positive feelings about another person simply *come out* in words!

- "I noticed something about you that I think is so strong . . ."
- "Got a minute? I want to tell you something I really appreciate about you."
- "I saw your post, and I have to tell you it made me appreciate how you . . ."
- "I know I don't tell you this enough, but you need to know that . . ."
- "After we talked the other day I want to thank you for being so . . ."
- "I admire that you know how to be . . ."

So often, we think these things of others but our good opinions stay in our heads. The Holy Spirit says, "Tell them!" When we do this, the root meaning and force of *encourage* comes to life—we infuse or put courage *into* someone!

The Father arranged special encouragement for the Son in his calling.

Jesus took with him Peter, James and John the brother of James, and led them up a high mountain by themselves.

There he was transfigured before them. His face shone
like the sun, and his clothes became as white as the light.
Just then there appeared before them Moses and Elijah,
talking with Jesus. . . .

While [Peter] was still speaking, a bright cloud
covered them, and a voice from the cloud said, "This is
my Son, whom I love; with him I am well pleased. Listen
to him!"

MATTHEW 17:1-3, 5, NIV

In contrast to Jesus' baptism, when virtually no ministry had taken
place, this encouragement from the Father to the Son followed a rig-
orous investment of time, travel, teaching, preaching, healing, and
training of the disciples. It's not a stretch at all to say that Jesus was
probably running on empty physically and emotionally. Our best
indicator that this was the case is that these words from the Father
were spoken in the context of Jesus *retreating* with the disciples. This
was his practice when he needed to refuel, and this was when God
chose to give him another special moment of encouragement.

Two men (Moses and Elijah) who, in their time, had been
tasked with intense earthly assignments by God, were present as
well. That was no accident! These guys knew all about stress. I
would love to have heard *that* conversation! Imagine Moses talking about going to Pharaoh or Elijah telling about confronting
the prophets of Baal. Can you imagine the two of them patting
Jesus on the back and encouraging him to stay the course, whatever his feelings at the moment? *This was a unique space, custom
built to encourage the Son.* While we don't know what was said,
we can strongly infer from the Father's encouraging and affirm-
ing words to his Son that the purpose that day was to encourage
Jesus in his journey with God and in his work for God. Jesus
literally "lit up"!

Jesus—empowered by the Holy Spirit—encouraged God's people at a critical moment to stay faithful, win the moment, and be rewarded.

> This is the message from the one who has the sevenfold Spirit of God and the seven stars: . . . "All who are victorious will be clothed in white. I will never erase their names from the Book of Life, but I will announce before my Father and his angels that they are mine."
> **REVELATION 3:1, 5, NLT**

It's as if Jesus, through the Holy Spirit, put his hand on John's shoulder as he wrote Revelation and said, "I need to get some strong encouragement to my followers. Take notes!" What follows is a simple pattern of encouragement, equipping, and edification custom-designed for believers encountering different struggles. By this example, we can learn from Jesus, working with the Holy Spirit, how to encourage other believers. Here's the blueprint:

- Recognize and celebrate their expressions of spiritual commitment.
- Review the specific obstacles or issues they are facing.
- Reignite their passion to *overcome* the obstacles in their path.
- Remind them of the reward if they are faithful.
- Remind them to actively *listen to the Holy Spirit* while on earth.

Spirit-empowered men give timely, powerful encouragement not to give up.

The men of Pentecost were sent specifically to encourage believers in person.

> Quite a number of the Greeks believed and turned to the Master.
>
> When the church in Jerusalem got wind of this, they sent Barnabas to Antioch to check on things. As soon as he arrived, he saw that God was behind and in it all. He threw himself in with them, got behind them, urging them to stay with it the rest of their lives.
>
> ACTS 11:21-23

In the midst of fluid and challenging moments of faith for many converted Jews and Gentiles, *in-person* encouragement was a powerful force for remaining faithful to Jesus. In person versus what? Versus by letter at the time, or today we would say in-person encouragement versus encouragement by email, text, or DM. Through Barnabas (a nickname meaning "son of encouragement"), we see that authentic and meaningful spiritual encouragement is genuinely joyful and on purpose. Following his example, when we come in contact with other believers, joy should pervade our spirits, and recognizing that all believers are at war, we should encourage them to hold on to their faith and fulfill their God-given purpose on earth.

The special ministry of encouragement is desperately needed to fight the good fight; this is as true now as it was when Acts was written. Otherwise, why would first-century believers go to the lengths they did to get a Spirit-empowered man on the first donkey to Antioch?

Through your encouraging presence, the Holy Spirit helps other believers "remain true to the Lord,"[3] doing whatever it takes to keep them out of despair and trusting God. The result? A vacuum in their spirit collapses. Without our encouragement, the evil one begins to fill the void and works to destroy our brothers and sisters in the Lord. Make no mistake, when we're facing pressure, temptation, persecution, or isolation, a fellow believer's encouragement becomes a spiritual weapon, and standing back-to-back, two can fight off *unfaithfulness* to God.

The Holy Spirit says, "It's urgent. Go encourage him!"

> See to it, brothers and sisters, that none of you has a sinful, unbelieving heart that turns away from the living God. But encourage one another daily, as long as it is called "Today," so that none of you may be hardened by sin's deceitfulness.[4]

Get this: a war is on to stop encouragement from flowing from believer to believer. Satan is well aware that under-encouraged believers free-fall into self-deception and unbelief. The Holy Spirit knows that encouragement is the oxygen of the believer's life. Without it, our faith dies—slowly and unnecessarily. That is why he ardently implores us *not* to critique or condemn other believers in his name. It is not a spiritual discipline to diminish their faith. It is a sign of insecurity.

Our job is to encourage our brothers and sisters so that we "strengthen what remains" (Revelation 3:2, NIV). Listen to the Holy Spirit through the words of Paul, pushing believers to engage in spiritual warfare by putting in the work of conflict resolution and entering into the ministry of encouragement: "Let us therefore make every effort to do what leads to peace and to mutual edification."[5]

Every effort versus what? Versus little or no effort. Spirit-empowered believers empower one another by edifying one another. This is where we get the word *edifice*. Followers of Jesus are like buildings that need support and buttressing with encouragement or else they will eventually crumble.

Making every effort to encourage means every effort counts.

Explosive Encouragement

So here are some concrete ways that a man of God makes every effort to get into the jet stream of encouragement by the Holy Spirit.

The Spirit-empowered man encourages believers in community.

> So let's *do* it—full of belief, confident that we're presentable inside and out. Let's keep a firm grip on the promises that keep us going. He always keeps his word. Let's see how inventive we can be in encouraging love and helping out, not avoiding worshiping together as some do but spurring each other on, especially as we see the big Day approaching.
> **HEBREWS 10:22-25**

There is no such thing as Holy Spirit encouragement without being in Holy Spirit community with other believers who are filled with the Holy Spirit!

If you are not in a spiritual community, you are—by default—under-encouraged spiritually. Consistency of connection is like the spiritual gas pump that fuels your spiritual engine, which in turn drives your efforts to love God and people. The Holy Spirit says, "STOP HERE" so you can both give and receive the encouragement he wants to pour out. Satan throws a lot of energy into making you apathetic or cynical about connecting with other believers, mainly because he knows that those connections will provide you with the encouragement you need to take a firm stand against his schemes. This means you have to look at community through a different lens—as essential to the fight for spiritual survival.

Fight for community! Win encouragement.

The Spirit-empowered man disciplines his will and words to encourage.

> Watch the way you talk. Let nothing foul or dirty come
> out of your mouth. Say only what helps, each word a gift.
> **EPHESIANS 4:29**

If you don't manage your mouth well, words come out that you can't put back in. You squeezed the toothpaste out! When that happens, exchanges between believers involve more active or passive tearing down and less active building up. Through your presence and your speech, the Holy Spirit wants to deliver targeted and helpful words that make other believers feel as if a gift is being given to fit their situation. Spirit-filled encouragement says no to unhelpful or self-serving comments in order to say yes to directed support. That is a tall order if you lack one crucial skill.

Encouraging well means listening well.

When you feel low, it is difficult to celebrate someone else's success. That's just a fact. But the man of God fights to celebrate another believer in the midst of his own failures and tough times; he knows God is working all things toward his perfect purpose. To do this, he must overcome jealousy, envy, conflicts, and personality differences through the healing work and security the Holy Spirit provides. He must also be with people long enough to know their needs and struggles in order to target life-giving encouragement.

God's got us, which means we have encouragement in reserve to offer without hesitation or reservation.

Fight for more encouraging words! Celebrate others, no matter what. God wins.

The Spirit-empowered man uses his spiritual gifts to encourage God's people.

> Since you are eager for gifts of the Spirit, try to excel in those that build up the church. . . . What then shall we say, brothers and sisters? When you come together, each of you has a hymn, or a word of instruction, a revelation, a tongue or an interpretation. Everything must be done so that the church may be built up.
>
> **1 CORINTHIANS 14:12, 26, NIV**

God has deposited some powerful tools in you that the Holy Spirit wants to use to encourage and strengthen your spiritual family. That's why they were given to you. Unfortunately, spiritual gifts can be used with selfish motives—to increase your visibility, to salve your insecurities, or to establish your spiritual superiority. Coach Paul had seen so many followers use their gifts for personal visibility, notoriety, and public piety, I imagine he wanted to throw up when he was accused of the same by some believers. It is hard to fight a perception, so he brought in God as his witness—the strongest possible invocation of integrity.

> Perhaps you think we're saying these things just to defend ourselves. No, we tell you this as Christ's servants, and with God as our witness. Everything we do, dear friends, is to strengthen you.[6]

The Holy Spirit imparts gifts to each believer, which are for the benefit of the body. But if a gift is polluted by pride, the believer harms the body of Christ. The Holy Spirit knows that a little knowledge is a very dangerous thing, so we must use the knowledge and insights we have been given to build others up according to their needs. Versus what? Building ourselves up according to our own needs.

Fight for the strength of the body of Christ!

The Holy Spirit gives believers a special commission to encourage other believers. No one else can provide this service to your brothers and sisters in Christ:

> Every bit of my commitment is for the purpose of building you up, after all, not tearing you down.[7]

In other words, a Christian is the Holy Spirit's sanctioned *ambassador of encouragement* to God's sons and daughters. He is looking for us to shoulder this responsibility personally, proudly, and powerfully to defeat discouragement and unfaithfulness in our spiritual families, just like my friend Lance did for me in the parking lot at church. In a very real way, *you* are your brother's keeper, as measured by your willingness to be used to encourage him.

Find a fellow believer to encourage today.

Holy Spirit,

Thank you for reminding me that in our family we encourage each other. Thank you for your uplifting works through your people. Help me to remember to use the gifts and skills you have given me to encourage others. Help me to listen well to other believers so I can encourage, celebrate, and strengthen them well. Help me to make every effort not to compete with other Christians but to connect with them to encourage their faithfulness to You. Heal the parts of me that cause me to withhold encouragement from others: the hurts, resentments, and insecurities that create jealousy, envy, division, and *personality conflicts. Love me out of those immature places of character so I can be free to encourage those around me, especially those who are followers of Jesus. From this place of freedom and healing in Christ, I accept my commission to exercise your authority to strengthen every believer I meet for his benefit and not my own. Thank you for this wonderful mission of giving encouragement to others. Fill me and use me to raise the spirits of my brothers and sisters, even as you have raised mine in Christ for the sake of the body. In Jesus' name, I pray. Amen.*

12

REACH SOMEONE'S SOUL

I Am a Soul Winner

"BRIAN, YOU NEED TO MEET THE MAN."

Slicing through the confusing "fat" of his phone conversation, my friend Kyle put the real issue on the table. He had spent the previous thirty minutes listening to a high school friend and former party buddy tell his story of hitting rock-bottom and deciding to get sober. Kyle had wanted to have a conversation like this with Brian (not his real name) for years, but this moment of great pain was the exact opportunity for Brian to experience God's Good News. There was maximum openness because a fresh wave of personal pain exceeded his fears and his pride.

Kyle listened intently to the painful circumstances in his old friend's life and, in the process, reflected on all the time the two shared surfing and partying hard. Many of the memories Kyle would just as soon forget, but others made him smile. Kyle used to be Brian's "brother from another mother." The fact that God would allow Kyle to be the one Brian called for spiritual advice seemed implausible, impossible, and comedic because of his past, but at the same time, that bond of shared past experiences made Kyle the perfect candidate.

So when Brian called, Kyle thought: *Thank you, Jesus.*

Brian lamented how his relationships were fragmenting, his career was disintegrating, and his mind was bending to the point of breaking. Kyle listened and reflected on the broken glass Brian's choices had made him crawl through and the hurt people left in his wake. It seemed so long ago that the evil combination of isolation from God and powerfully destructive appetites had enslaved him. Brian's story jogged his memory and reminded him *exactly* how far he had come because of "the Man" who came into his life at his own rock-bottom. He remembered the day, the hour, the church, and most importantly, the freedom he felt in that moment when the Holy Spirit invaded and, through Christ, healed three decades of loneliness and addiction.

Brian turned a corner at about the twentieth minute of the phone call and started to talk about how he'd come home to an empty house two weeks prior and found all traces of his beautiful wife and four kids missing. Closets emptied, drawers left pulled out, toothbrushes not in the holders, the minivan's space in the garage empty, and Jackie's wedding ring on the dresser next to a short note in her familiar script. Brian was now officially alone.

Sitting on the floor in his youngest daughter's room, Brian read Jackie's note through a vodka-induced stupor. She loved him, but she was done. It felt like a building collapsing on top of him. For Brian, that moment was the epiphany Jackie had attempted to help him see through years of arguing about Brian's drinking. In his haze he remembered the faces of his children. *What would he do without them?* Despite this painful new reality, Brian was unwilling to have a father's suicide be the legacy he left his kids. He loved his family, but he didn't know what to do.

Brian had no other choice but to fight for his life. The first step was to completely cut off a very old mistress—alcohol. Brian went to his first two Alcoholics Anonymous meetings and, though he was horribly uncomfortable, he also knew *that was the point*. He was utterly humiliated by his own actions with no defense other than to accept responsibility.

Brian shared his AA experience with Kyle. This is when the conversation turned spiritual.

> **Brian:** *This is a spiritual program, Kyle. They are talking about God "as I understand him," and I don't even have an "understanding" to get started with that one. You were the first person I thought of calling. You have been down this path and seem to know how to do this. What do I do?*

The Holy Spirit was already moving ahead of Kyle and knew the exact way for him to relay the next spiritual step to his friend. Brian simply needed an introduction to Christ, and my brother was going to make that introduction in a way that Brian would receive it.

> **Kyle:** *Brian, you need to meet the Man.*

Drawing the Net

The Holy Spirit is fighting for souls and is responsible for wooing people and animating salvation moments—sealing a permanent relationship with God. Having a strong relationship and partnership with the Holy Spirit means working with him in his mission to connect the love of God to the people he has placed in your life.

Social scientists say the average man in his mid-twenties will reach out to nineteen friends a month out of the network of two hundred-plus contacts he interfaces with in some way on a weekly basis.[1] Pause and ponder that. Think about the people the Holy Spirit is seeking to touch right now in your everyday life!

- Immediate and extended family members
- Network of all your friends (think of the contacts in your phone alone)
- Coworkers
- Neighbors
- Hobby or recreational communities
- Parents connected to kids' activities
- Coaches
- Teachers
- Baristas
- **Every person with whom you have regular contact**

As the Holy Spirit is forming a Christlike attitude in you, he equips and prepares you to battle as Jesus did for the eternal future of those he has placed in your life. Think of a fisherman who casts his net in a specific, target-rich area of water. The net must be drawn to catch a good haul of fish. Right now, God is taking all the relationships and connections he has placed in your life and putting that *net* to *work*. See what I did there? Your *network* is the Holy Spirit's to use to reach souls. It is uniquely yours in the life you are living—in the place where you work, in the space where you play, and in the fellowships where you pray. So what is the Holy Spirit doing within you to impact these spaces right now?

The Holy Spirit is moving us to sacrifice for the lost by being like Christ.

Suppose one of you had a hundred sheep and lost one. Wouldn't you leave the ninety-nine in the wilderness and

go after the lost one until you found it? When found,
you can be sure you would put it across your shoulders,
rejoicing, and when you got home call in your friends
and neighbors, saying, "Celebrate with me! I've found my
lost sheep!"

LUKE 15:4-6

Attempting to reach someone's soul requires a decision on
your part and is usually synonymous with a momentary
inconvenience. You have to leave someone or something in order
to make another person the focus of your spiritual attention.
You have to leave the emotional safety zone of acceptance for
the risk-filled world of possible rejection. You might be called
to cross cultural, political, or personal boundaries to gain an
audience with someone.

When Jesus talked about leaving the wilderness to go after a
lost sheep, he meant leaving the flat ground for the hilly, the easy
path for the hard, the safe terrain for the unsafe. Today, leaving
the wilderness could take us to a new country or environment
where Christ's love has not been shared before. Leaving what you
know, who you are comfortable with, and where you are known
to be with someone who has not received the person and work
of Christ for themselves is to "leave the ninety-nine . . . and go
after the lost one."

Wherever lost sheep are, the Holy Spirit will lead us to them.

**The Holy Spirit will use our conversations to testify about
Christ in our lives.**

When the Friend I plan to send you from the Father
comes—the Spirit of Truth issuing from the Father—he
will confirm everything about me. You, too, from your

side must give your confirming evidence, since you are in
this with me from the start.
JOHN 15:26-27

We talk about what we are truly excited about. This includes gadgets that make our lives easier, apparel we love, restaurants that serve amazing food and drinks, and just about anything that enriches our lives. When we do that, *we are the best evidence* for whatever we are evangelizing to someone else! Think about all the things or places we tell others "you have to try!" Cooperating with the Holy Spirit is synonymous with talking often about the person of Jesus *if* we are truly animated and convinced about his presence in our lives. And while many interactions we have throughout the day are incidental or transactional by nature, many others can be eternal and monumental if we are in close contact with the Holy Spirit.

Think of the people God is calling you to get closer to *within the flow of your life* so they will consider the claims of Christ. Jesus' point above is simple and challenging: if a relationship is truly meaningful to you, *you can't* not *talk about it with others.*

The Holy Spirit prompts us to know and make known the clear terms of the gospel.

I passed on to you what was most important and what had also been passed on to me. Christ died for our sins, just as the Scriptures said. He was buried, and he was raised from the dead on the third day, just as the Scriptures said.
1 CORINTHIANS 15:3-4, NLT, EMPHASIS MINE

The Holy Spirit prompts followers who are concerned about the lost to distill the message about Jesus to the point where they are comfortable sharing it with others. It starts with your testimony and what you believed when you came to Christ—nailing that, and then giving others the same message for them to trust.

Coach Paul says this is the fundamental, or "most important," message all followers must eventually communicate when having a conversation with someone about salvation. Why? Because that is what they receive by faith in order to begin and eternally continue a relationship with God. They receive Christ as Lord (God) and Savior (the one who died for their sin and rescued them from judgment).

Salvation is found uniquely in the person and work of Christ. More personally and practically, simply ask yourself:

- What was my personal *aha* regarding Jesus that made the light bulb turn on inside and allowed me to turn from myself and my sin to embrace the person of Jesus Christ?
- What did the Holy Spirit clear up for me?
- Why did it make sense then and not before?
- Why was it so meaningful?
- How did the information *about* Jesus turn into *a relationship* with Jesus?"
- Which of my friends do I want to introduce to Jesus?

These are all questions the Holy Spirit has already answered in your life. The most natural thing we can do is to share the clarity he has given us with others.

The Holy Spirit prompts us to persuade others to consider Jesus Christ.

It's no light thing to know that we'll all one day stand in that place of Judgment. *That's why we work urgently with everyone we meet to get them ready to face God.*
2 CORINTHIANS 5:10-11, EMPHASIS MINE

The Holy Spirit impresses upon us the importance of seeking a person's best possible future. That means we meaningfully and sincerely initiate conversations about Jesus with others—because we love them! Work hard to follow the Holy Spirit's lead as he uses you to persuade others about Jesus. This means being alert to opportunities to listen to people and pray for them, and in general being sensitive to the guidance of the Holy Spirit. Above all, it involves taking relational and personal risks to move those you talk to toward the person of Jesus Christ in the best way possible.

The Holy Spirit will validate for others the truth of the gospel message.

> Once people have seen the light, gotten a taste of heaven and *been part of the work of the Holy Spirit*, . . . they can't start over as if nothing happened. That's impossible.
> **HEBREWS 6:4-6, EMPHASIS MINE**

> When he comes, he will prove the world to be in the wrong about sin and righteousness and judgment: about sin, because people do not believe in me; about righteousness, because I am going to the Father, where you can see me no longer; and about judgment, because the prince of this world now stands condemned.
> **JOHN 16:8-11, NIV**

The best news ever is that the Holy Spirit's job is to take what you say and make it sing! It is called *convicting a person*. That means the Holy Spirit's job (not ours) is to move them into an awareness of God, a consciousness of their need, and a clear understanding of what they have to do—repent from self-sufficiency and come to God humbly and dependently. You and I can't change anyone's thoughts toward God, assuage deep-seated cynicisms, or heal past traumas that cause them to question God's existence.

When you think of the Holy Spirit in your life, you cannot divorce yourself from his desire to *draw the net* as he fishes for men willing to be used to bring people to salvation and full fellowship with Jesus. He is eager, on the job, good at convicting the heart, and knows the absolute best way to bring the message home.

And if you have prayed and prayed for another person and are ready to throw in the towel—don't. Instead, be praying for the Holy Spirit to open that person's heart to God *his way* and be ready to help when the right time comes. If there is one thing I have learned in over four decades of sharing Jesus with people, it is that the Holy Spirit's methods of softening and cracking open the human heart to receive the gospel are numerous, sometimes bizarre, and always just right.

The Holy Spirit says, "Do not stop praying." Pray Jesus' prayer.

> Father, it's time.
> Display the bright splendor of your Son
> So the Son in turn may show your bright splendor.
> You put him in charge of everything human
> So he might give real and eternal life to all in his care.
> And this is the real and eternal life:
> That they know you,
> The one and only true God,
> And Jesus Christ, whom you sent.[2]

Mysterious Perfection

The Holy Spirit is a creative opportunist.

The twists and turns of Don's story are still fresh in my mind.

Wild. Crazy. Out there. But true and documented. Follow it with me for the first time, putting yourself in his shoes, like I did.

Imagine spending a year in the jungles of Papua, New Guinea, painstakingly documenting and learning the language of an indigenous tribe that had never before seen a missionary. Your assignment: earn their acceptance, establish a friendly presence, learn the customs, and learn the language so that you can tell them the story of Jesus. All of this takes thousands of interactive events and a quick pen and pad—but you are successful.

You have to merge the languages of the Bible with their native tongue, assign the right vocabulary words, connect the storylines across the cultures, and deliver the gospel for the indigenous people to either accept or reject in their own context. The work of translation is difficult, but after asking many questions about the accuracy of your new translation, you feel the story of Jesus has been rendered well and will be understood by this tribe. It's time to ask the elders for a gathering to talk of the Creator and his plan for all people. Your request is granted, the big moment arrives, and while nervous at first, you begin communicating the story of Jesus from the Gospel of John by saying, "In the beginning was the voice of God."

Even you are surprised at how intrigued the people are with your story about Jesus upon hearing of him for the first time. They are listening intently, reacting, and talking to each other as they hear of the different events surrounding the "Son of Creator" who has a funny name. They are *dialed in* and want to hear more about the miracle man who heals people and talks of his Father-Creator. You could not be more pleased with how the whole process is going.

Over the next week, your journey through John's Gospel takes the people from Jesus' arrival on earth to his parables, to the garden of Gethsemane, right through to his betrayal by Judas, his trial before the council, his death, and his resurrection. Exhausted, relieved, and eager for a response, it is time for you to hear their reaction.

After the final storytelling gathering, the tribal elder says that the story of the Son of Creator was good and that there was a part of the story they were particularly excited about. You cannot wait to hear about their positive connection to the gospel. "That is," he continues, "the excellent work of Judas in betraying the Son of Creator with a kiss of death and getting him to the men who would nail him to a cross." The man Judas, in their opinion, is the hero, and Jesus is the weak one for letting himself be tricked by a *skilled* betrayer!

A year of painstaking work for *"Hail Judas"*?

I listened with rapt attention as Don Richardson described this true but discouraging story of heartbreak on the mission field. *Brutal, dude,* I thought. As it turned out, the Sawi tribe Richardson had befriended idealized violence through trickery! As Don continued describing this culture of revenge, I thought his takeaway would be "faithfulness in the midst of fruitlessness" or a pep talk on endurance and hanging in there for the gospel, no matter what.

In other words, the Sawi would not be transformed by the gospel.

Thankfully, this was not the case, as Don told how in the Holy Spirit's hands, *the very thing* that drove the Sawi away from Jesus toward Judas became *the very thing* that brought them back to saving faith in Christ: *violence.*

One day a discouraged Don observed a Sawi child being taken to a rival tribe. He asked why one of their own babies was being forced to live among their enemies. The tribesman explained to Don that if a child was offered as a "peace gift" from one tribe to another, conflicts between those tribes would never be settled violently. The Holy Spirit pounced on this and was waiting to show Don the opening. Fortunately, his Holy Spirit radar was "on," so he started to ponder what he was observing:

- A son is offered by the chief of one tribe to another.
- As long as the child lives with the other tribe, disputes are settled without violence and a condition of peace prevails.
- The son replaces vengeance toward one another in the minds of the people.
- No true peace is possible without the gift of a peace child.

Then the Holy Spirit whacked Don over the head with this insight: *a peace child . . . Jesus . . . making peace between man and God!*

Richardson went back to his dwelling for the next few days and reframed the story of Jesus in the context of the peace child custom. When he re-presented the story of the Son of Creator to the Sawi, this time the tribesmen responded positively, realizing the Father-Creator had *but one Son* and Jesus was offered as a peace child. The whole tribe converted to Christianity from a violent brand of animism.[3]

> He has made everything beautiful in its time. He has also set eternity in the human heart; yet no one can fathom what God has done from beginning to end.[4]

God made every person to live for eternity, but an active campaign to thwart God's intention rages. You and I are called to take every opportunity presented to us by the Holy Spirit to make connections between the gospel and the real-life issues in the lives of the people we know and encounter. We pray before contact, asking the Holy Spirit to prepare someone's mind to hear the truth of the gospel. We pray in the moment, asking the Holy Spirit to place in our minds the best way to deliver the gospel to their heart. We pray after an encounter, asking the Holy Spirit to make connections in their mind to confirm the reality of Jesus' person and work for them on the cross. The Holy Spirit delights in our passion for the lost, our willing cooperation with him, our authentic conversation, and our available spirit.

> Pray diligently. Stay alert, with your eyes wide open in gratitude. Don't forget to pray for us, that God will open doors for telling the mystery of Christ. . . . Pray that every time I open my mouth I'll be able to make Christ plain as day to them.
> Use your heads as you live and work among outsiders. Don't miss a trick. Make the most of every opportunity. Be gracious in your speech. The goal is to bring out the best in others in a conversation, not put them down, not cut them out.[5]

The best way to be a witness and give evidence of the hope that is in you is to allow the Holy Spirit to provide you with the intel, the opportunity, the clarity, the relevancy, and the integrity of connection that people deserve.

The Holy Spirit who used the pain of a wife and family leaving (Kyle's friend Brian) and the Holy Spirit who used a bizarre tribal custom of giving a precious baby away to live with an enemy tribe is the same Holy Spirit who knows exactly how to make the message of the gospel resonate with those he places around us. We simply need to stay prayerful, stay available, and stay faithful to a door of opportunity, knowing that he is *way ahead of us.*

From Fear to Total Freedom

The Holy Spirit moves men from fear to total freedom in sharing the Good News, as the first followers experienced firsthand in the place where they were living, working, praying, and playing.

With that, Peter, full of the Holy Spirit, let loose: "Rulers and leaders of the people, if we have been brought to trial today for helping a sick man, put under investigation regarding this healing, I'll be completely frank with you— we have nothing to hide. By the name of Jesus Christ of Nazareth, the One you killed on a cross, the One God raised from the dead, by means of his name this man stands before you healthy and whole. Jesus is 'the stone you masons threw out, which is now the cornerstone.' Salvation comes no other way; no other name has been or will be given to us by which we can be saved, only this one."[6]

The Spirit was set loose in Peter's world and is now being set loose in yours.

Peter's journey from fright to fearlessness is a testament to what the Holy Spirit wants to do *in us in our unique context*. Filled with the Holy Spirit, Peter was no longer living for an audience of many but an audience of One. This is witnessed by his total lack of concern *for others he once feared would harm him if he spoke up as a follower*—the people pleaser was now a God-pleaser and God-fearer. The difference between Peter A and Peter B is a fresh filling and empowering by the Holy Spirit.

The result? *No fear*. This is what Peter did:

- He drew attention away from himself.
- He pointed his audience to Christ.
- He gave credit to God for the work they had seen.
- He clearly addressed their actions.
- He clearly stated the gospel.
- He left no wiggle room.

Peter's next sermon to this group got him a flogging and an order from the local authorities "not to speak in Jesus' name."[7]

That, too, was met by a total lack of concern, as the overflow of Peter and his community of followers kept spreading from their insides out to their world. The no from religious authorities backfired totally. The community of first followers took it as a sign they were on the right track and as an emphatic yes from God.

> The apostles went out of the High Council overjoyed
> because they had been given the honor of being
> dishonored on account of the Name. Every day they were
> in the Temple and homes, teaching and preaching Christ
> Jesus, not letting up for a minute.[8]

So much fear before the coming of the Holy Spirit—so much freedom after his powerful, fresh wind ignited the kindling in their souls.

As I have mentioned repeatedly, the good news *about* the Good News is that the Holy Spirit is way ahead of us, already working in the hearts and minds of those we are called to reach for Jesus. It's like being in on a surprise party, except this one is the surprise party to end all surprise parties! The goal here is not pressure but peace in the pre-workings of the Holy Spirit and to faithfully do what only you can do *so that the Holy Spirit can do what only he can do.*

Coach Paul—one of the best ambassadors of the gospel ever—passed along the secret to being used by the Holy Spirit to reach a soul:

> You'll remember, friends, that when I first came to you to
> let you in on God's sheer genius, I didn't try to impress
> you with polished speeches and the latest philosophy. I
> deliberately kept it plain and simple: first Jesus and who
> he is; then Jesus and what he did—Jesus crucified.
>
> I was unsure of how to go about this, and felt totally
> inadequate—I was scared to death, if you want the truth

of it—and so nothing I said could have impressed you or anyone else. But the Message came through anyway. God's Spirit and God's power did it, which made it clear that your life of faith is a response to God's power, not to some fancy mental or emotional footwork by me or anyone else.[9]

Do you see it? The Holy Spirit's *less is more* approach to reaching souls is tried and true:

- You take the initiative to go to others *("when I first came")*.
- You intentionally keep your testimony and message simple *("Jesus and what he did")*.
- You let the Holy Spirit take the loaves and fish of your obedience and multiply them into the salvation and transformation of others' lives *("God's Spirit and God's power did it")*.

God is asking you to play a part in the overarching tale of the Kingdom of God, presented to an enormous, Holy-Spirit-prepared-and-receptive audience. And just like we need to eat to sustain our physical energy, the Holy Spirit says we need to fill up on God's purposes in this hour because the table is set for us. A fire is ready to fall, fill, overflow, and spread. Like Jesus did with his disciples before returning to the Father, the Holy Spirit is calling you to work with him to reach souls uniquely connected to your life.

The Holy Spirit says, "Let his attitude be your attitude."

Jesus said, "The food that keeps me going is that I do the will of the One who sent me, finishing the work he started. As you look around right now, wouldn't you say that in about four months it will be time to harvest? Well, I'm telling you to open your eyes and take a good look at what's right in front of you. These Samaritan fields are ripe. It's harvest time!

"The Harvester isn't waiting. He's taking his pay, gathering in this grain that's ripe for eternal life. Now the Sower is arm in arm with the Harvester, triumphant."[10]

Our final prayer:

Holy Spirit,

Thank you for this journey of discovering how you intend to fill me, change me, overflow out of me, and spread the Kingdom of God. I want to be salt, I want to be light, and I want to be the aroma that spreads the knowledge of Christ everywhere I go. This is your intention for me, and I surrender to my identity, your prompting, and your manifesting of supernatural expression through me. Help me to be alert in new ways to what you are doing and guide me in playing my part as you work in the lives of others. I want to join you in the process. Help me to be an agent of your power, an ambassador, and to share with others my hope in Christ through the gospel. Give me your eyes to see people the way you see them—as precious ones needing to know and experience God's love; lost ones needing to find their refuge in their Maker and Savior; lonely ones who need to find hope again, have their past forgiven, and find purpose for living; and deceived ones who need to know the truth and experience freedom and healing deep within. Use me. Grab my heart. Grip my emotions. Open my mouth. Light a new fire within, and set me loose to serve you until I die. In Jesus' name I ask. Amen.

APPENDIX A

THE EMPOWERING PRESENCE

WHICH OF THE WORDS listed below would you use to describe your current experience as a follower of Jesus? (Circle those that apply to you.)

Growing	Dynamic	Discouraged	Defeated
Fulfilled	So-so	Mediocre	Synthetic
Struggling	Frustrated	Guilty	Duty
Exciting	Forgiven	Lifeless	Painful
Empty	Joyful	Disappointing	Vital
Intimate	Up and down	Stuck	Authentic

Do You Desire More?

Jesus said, "Let anyone who is thirsty come to me and drink. Whoever believes in me, as Scripture has said, rivers of living water will flow from within them."[1] What did Jesus mean? John, the biblical author, went on to explain, "By this he meant the Spirit, whom those who believed in him were later to receive. Up to that time the Spirit had not been given, since Jesus had not yet been glorified."[2]

Jesus promised that the Holy Spirit would satisfy the thirst, or deepest longings, of all who believe in him. However, many Christians do not understand the Holy Spirit or how to experience him in their daily lives. The following principles will help you understand and enjoy the Holy Spirit.

The divine gift

God has given us his Spirit so that we can experience intimacy with him and enjoy all he has for us. The Holy Spirit is the source of our deepest satisfaction. The Holy Spirit is God's permanent presence with us.

Jesus said, "And I will ask the Father, and he will give you another advocate to help you and be with you forever—the Spirit of truth."[3]

The Holy Spirit enables us to understand and experience all God has given us.

> What we have received is not the spirit of the world, but
> the Spirit who is from God, so that we may understand
> what God has freely given us.[4]

The Holy Spirit enables us to experience many things:

- A genuine new spiritual life (John 3:1-8)
- The assurance of being a child of God (Romans 8:15-16)
- The infinite love of God (Romans 5:5; Ephesians 3:16-19)

The present danger

Why are many Christians not satisfied in their experience with God?

Experiencing intimacy with God and enjoying all he has for us hinges on our connection and partnership with his Spirit. People who trust in their own efforts and strength to live the Christian life will experience failure and frustration, as will those who live to please themselves rather than God.

We cannot live the Christian life in our own strength.

> Are you so foolish? After beginning by means of the
> Spirit, are you now trying to finish by means of the flesh?[5]

We cannot enjoy all God desires for us if we live by our self-centered desires.

> For the flesh desires what is contrary to the Spirit,
> and the Spirit what is contrary to the flesh. They are
> in conflict with each other, so that you are not to do
> whatever you want.[6]

> The person without the Spirit does not accept the things
> that come from the Spirit of God but considers them
> foolishness, and cannot understand them because they are
> discerned only through the Spirit.[7]

> The person with the Spirit makes judgments about all
> things. . . . We have the mind of Christ.[8]

> But those who are controlled by the Holy Spirit think
> about things that please the Spirit.[9]

Walking together in God

How can we develop a lifestyle of depending on the Spirit?

By walking in the Spirit, we increasingly experience intimacy with God and enjoy all he has for us. As we walk in the Spirit, we have the ability to live a life pleasing to God.

> So I say, walk by the Spirit, and you will not gratify the desires of the flesh. . . . Since we live by the Spirit, let us keep in step with the Spirit.[10]

> But the fruit of the Spirit is love, joy, peace, forbearance, kindness, goodness, faithfulness, gentleness and self-control.[11]

Spiritual breathing is a powerful word picture that can help you experience moment-by-moment dependence upon the Spirit.

Exhale: Confess your sin the moment you become aware of it. Agree with God concerning it, and thank him for his forgiveness, according to 1 John 1:9 and Hebrews 10:1-25. Confession requires repentance—a change in attitude and action.

Inhale: Surrender control of your life to Christ, and rely upon the Holy Spirit to fill you with *his presence* and *his power* by faith, according to *his command* (Ephesians 5:18) and *his promise* (1 John 5:14-15).

Three Important Questions to Ask Yourself:

1. *Am I ready to surrender control of my life to Jesus Christ?*
2. *Am I ready to confess my sins (1 John 1:9)?* Sin grieves God's Spirit (Ephesians 4:30). But God in his love has forgiven all of your sins—past, present, and future—because Christ died for you.
3. *Do I sincerely desire to be directed and empowered by the Holy Spirit (John 7:37-39)?*

By faith you can now claim the fullness of the Spirit according to his command and promise:

God **COMMANDS** us to be filled with the Spirit.

> Don't be drunk with wine, because that will ruin your life. Instead, be filled with the Holy Spirit.[12]

God **PROMISES** he will always answer when we pray according to his will.

> This is the confidence we have in approaching God: that if we ask anything according to his will, he hears us. And if we know that he hears us—whatever we ask—we know that we have what we asked of him.[13]

The turning point

Honest prayer is a strong way of expressing our faith. The following is a suggested prayer:

> *Dear Father,*
>
> *I need you. I acknowledge that I have sinned against you by directing my own life. I thank you that you have forgiven my sins through Christ's death on the cross for me. I now invite Christ to again take his place on the throne of my life. Fill me with the Holy Spirit as you commanded me to be filled and as you promised in your Word that you would do if I asked in faith. I pray this in the name of Jesus. I now thank you for filling me with the Holy Spirit and directing my life.*

Does this prayer express the desire of your heart?

If so, you can pray right now and trust God to fill you with his Holy Spirit.

GOOD QUESTIONS: *How can I know that I am filled by the Holy Spirit?*
    Did I ask God to fill me with the Holy Spirit?
    Do I know that I am now filled with the Holy Spirit?
    On what authority do I know I am filled?

A GOOD ANSWER: On the trustworthiness of God himself and his Word, according to Romans 5:5 and Ezekiel 36:27.

As you continue to depend on God's Spirit moment by moment, you will experience a truly rich and satisfying life in Christ.

Now that you are filled with the Holy Spirit, thank God that the Spirit will enable you:

- To glorify Christ with your life (John 16:13-14)
- To grow in your understanding of God and his Word
  (1 Corinthians 2:14-16)
- To live a life pleasing to God (Galatians 5:16-23)

Finally, remember the promise of Jesus about his empowering presence:

> But you will receive power when the Holy Spirit comes
> on you; and you will be my witnesses in Jerusalem, and in
> all Judea and Samaria, and to the ends of the earth.[14]

APPENDIX B

TRULY DIFFERENT, TRULY GOOD

Claiming the Fullness of the Spirit

THIS APPENDIX HIGHLIGHTS some specific ideas for how we can give the Holy Spirit more capacity to shine through us.

Do everything without grumbling or arguing (Philippians 2:14-15).
Believe in and follow Jesus (John 8:12).
Be countercultural in Christ (Romans 12:1-2).
Live uniquely to please God alone (John 8:28-29).
React compassionately to injustice (John 8:1-11).
Serve people (Luke 22:25-27).
Be radically generous when God tells you to be (Proverbs 11:25).
Put yourself "out there" to connect with people (1 Corinthians 9:19-23).
Control your mouth (James 3:8).

Use your mouth to build others up (Ephesians 4:29).

Be consistent (Colossians 3:17).

Deliver excellence in your work and attitude (Colossians 3:23).

Say no to yourself to say yes to others (John 15:13).

Be a Golden Rule follower (Luke 6:31).

Listen really well and ask the next question (James 1:19).

Go the second mile (Matthew 5:41).

Be honest with yourself and others (Proverbs 28:13).

Know God's Word (Ezra 7:10; Psalm 119:165).

Live with eternal urgency (John 9:4-5).

Risk for the gospel (Mark 8:35).

Practice hospitality and bless people (Romans 12:13).

Serve the least of these and the lonely (Matthew 25:34-36).

Offer kindness and gentleness (Colossians 3:13).

Forgive and show mercy (Micah 6:8).

Bless others with your presence and prayers (Romans 12:15).

NOTES

INTRODUCTION: THE OVERARCHING TALE

1. "Highest Grossing Film Franchises and Series Worldwide as of August 2021," Statista, August 27, 2021, https://www.statista.com/statistics /317408/highest-grossing-film-franchises-series/.
2. Sarah Darmanjian, "These Are the Top Halloween Costumes of 2021, According to One Survey," *News Nation*, updated October 3, 2021, https://www.newsnationnow.com/us-news/these-are-the-top-halloween -costumes-of-2021-according-to-one-survey/.
3. Alyssa Meyers and Sarah Shevenock, "Is Gen Z Too Cool for Marvel? Just 9% of Marvel Fans Identify as Part of the Generation," December 6, 2021, https://morningconsult.com/2021/12/06/is-gen-z-too-cool-for-marvel/.
4. Ecclesiastes 3:11, NLT.
5. John 14:12, NIV, emphasis mine.
6. John 7:37-39, NIV.
7. Acts 1:8, NIV.
8. Mark 8:34-37, NLT.
9. *Merriam-Webster*, s.v. "fill," https://www.merriam-webster.com /dictionary/fill.
10. John 20:20-22.
11. *Merriam-Webster*, s.v. "overflow," https://www.merriam-webster.com /dictionary/overflow.
12. Acts 4:13-16.
13. *Merriam-Webster*, s.v. "spread," https://www.merriam-webster.com /dictionary/spread.
14. Acts 8:25.
15. Romans 8:19, NASB1995.
16. 1 John 5:14-15, NIV.

CHAPTER 1: SALT BY CONTACT

1. Matthew 5:13.
2. "Sodium Chloride," Healthline, updated August 18, 2016, https://www .healthline.com/health/sodium-chloride.
3. Colossians 4:6, NIV.
4. Matthew 10:8, NIV.
5. Romans 5:15, NIV.
6. 2 Corinthians 4:13-15.
7. Wim Hordijk, "From Salt to Salary: Linguists Take a Page from Science," November 8, 2014, https://www.npr.org/sections/13.7/2014/11/08 /362478685/from-salt-to-salary-linguists-take-a-page-from-science.
8. Mark 9:50.
9. Matthew 10:12-13, NIV.
10. Matthew 5:9.
11. 1 Peter 3:10-12.
12. Leviticus 2:13.
13. 2 Chronicles 13:4-7.
14. Luke 6:46, NIV.
15. John 15:13-14, NIV.
16. Galatians 2:19-21.
17. 2 Corinthians 5:15, NLT.
18. Genesis 19:26.
19. Deuteronomy 29:23.
20. Judges 9:45.
21. Psalm 33:5, NIV.
22. 1 Peter 3:12, NIV.
23. Matthew 16:18-19, NIV.
24. Matthew 6:13, KJV.
25. 1 John 3:7-8, NIV.
26. Mark 9:43-50, NIV.
27. Matthew 5:13, NIV.
28. Matthew 5:13, NIV.
29. John 15:18-19, NIV.
30. Luke 4:5-8, NIV.
31. Luke 4:13, NIV.

CHAPTER 2: LIGHT BY CONTRAST

1. Mark 8:35, NLT.
2. Luke 7:36-39, 44-47, NIV.
3. Matthew 5:14-16.
4. John 8:12, NIV.
5. Isaiah 9:2, 6, NLT.

6. John 3:19-21.
7. John 12:46, NIV.
8. John 1:4, NIV.
9. 1 Thessalonians 5:5-8.
10. Acts 17:26-27, NIV.
11. 1 Corinthians 7:17.
12. Philippians 2:12-16.
13. 2 Timothy 2:4-6, NIV.
14. Matthew 12:33-35, NLT.
15. Jeremiah 2:13, NLT.
16. Matthew 5:15-16.
17. Luke 11:34-36, NLT.
18. For example, see Genesis 3:1 and Judges 16:20.
19. Luke 11:35, NLT.
20. Luke 11:36, NLT.
21. 1 John 1:5-10.

CHAPTER 3: AROMA THAT SPREADS

1. "How Perfume Affects the Brain: Your Powerful Sense of Smell and Memory," *Herb & Root*, accessed May 25, 2022, https://herbandroot.com/blogs/self-love/how-perfume-affects-the-brain.
2. "Roman Triumph—Background—The *vir Triumphalis*," *Liquisearch*, accessed May 25, 2022, https://www.liquisearch.com/roman_triumph/background/the_vir_triumphalis.
3. Philip J. Long, "A Captive in Christ's Triumphal Procession—2 Corinthians 2:12-17," *Reading Acts*, October 9, 2019, https://readingacts.com/2019/10/09/a-captive-in-christs-triumphal-procession-2-corinthians-212-17/.
4. 1 John 5:4-5.
5. 1 John 4:17, NIV.
6. Romans 8:29-30.
7. 1 Thessalonians 5:11.
8. Ephesians 2:1-2, NLT.
9. 1 Thessalonians 2:15-16.
10. Matthew 13:24-30, NLT, emphasis mine.
11. Matthew 11:28-30, NLT.
12. Micah 6:8, NIV.
13. Luke 11:35, NLT.
14. Matthew 23:23-24, NIV.
15. Matthew 23:25-26, NIV.
16. Matthew 23:27-28, NIV.
17. 1 Samuel 16:7, NIV.

18. Cathleen Falsani, *The God Factor: Inside the Spiritual Lives of Public People* (New York: Sarah Crichton Books, 2006), 11.

CHAPTER 4: AVAILABLE TO GOD IN MY CONTEXT

1. Colossians 3:1-2.
2. 2 Corinthians 4:18, NIV.
3. Ephesians 5:15-20, NIV.
4. Ezekiel 22:30.
5. Galatians 5:22-25, NIV.
6. Galatians 5:25, NIV.
7. Acts 8:26-38, NIV.
8. Matthew 11:19, NIV.
9. Luke 4:18-19, NLT.
10. 1 Corinthians 9:19-23.
11. 2 Timothy 2:20-21.

CHAPTER 5: PRAYERFUL TO GOD IN MY CONTEXT

1. Charles M. Province, "George Patton's Address to the Troops," *The Patton Society*, accessed May 18, 2022, http://www.pattonhq.com/speech.html.
2. History.com Editors, "George S. Patton," *History*, updated April 28, 2020, https://www.history.com/topics/world-war-ii/george-smith-patton.
3. History on the Net Editors, "Patton's Entrance into Germany in 1945," *History on the Net*, accessed May 19, 2022, https://www.historyonthenet .com/pattons-entrance-into-germany-in-1945.
4. Matthew 11:12, NLT.
5. 2 Corinthians 10:3-8, NLT.
6. Ephesians 6:10-18.
7. Luke 10:1-3, 17-21.
8. Luke 9:1-5.
9. Acts 3:16, NIV.
10. Acts 4:13-18, NASB1995.
11. Ephesians 1:19-22; 2:6, NLT.
12. Matthew 16:18-19, NIV.
13. John 14:12-14, NIV.
14. Matthew 6:9-13, NIV.
15. 1 John 5:13-15.
16. Ephesians 6:12, KJV.

CHAPTER 6: FAITHFUL TO GOD IN MY CONTEXT

1. Andrew Bisharat, "Why Are So Many BASE Jumpers Dying?" *National Geographic*, August 30, 2016, https://www.nationalgeographic.com /adventure/article/why-are-so-many-base-jumpers-dying.

2. Ibid.
3. Allison Linn, "Hundreds of Suppliers, One Boeing 737 Airplane," NBC News, April 27, 2010, https://www.nbcnews.com/id/wbna36507420.
4. Mark 8:35, NLT.
5. Ephesians 2:10.
6. Hebrews 10:38-39, NIV.
7. Isaiah 5:7, NASB1995.
8. Matthew 17:1-5.
9. Hebrews 11:1-2.
10. Hebrews 12:1-3.
11. Matthew 25:23, NLT.
12. Hebrews 11:6.
13. John 9:4-5.
14. Matthew 6:19-21.
15. Galatians 6:9-10, NIV.
16. Hebrews 12:11.
17. *Merriam-Webster*, s.v. "opportunity," https://www.merriam-webster.com /dictionary/opportunity.
18. *The Britannica Dictionary*, s.v. "opportunity," https://www.britannica.com /dictionary/opportunity.
19. Colossians 4:5-6.
20. 1 Corinthians 16:7-9, NLT.
21. Matthew 12:33-35, NLT.
22. Romans 15:13-15, NLT.

CHAPTER 7: SETTING THE HOLY SPIRIT LOOSE

1. George Pararas-Carayannis, "The Great Explosion of the Krakatau Volcano ('Krakatoa') of August 26, 1883, in Indonesia," *Disaster Pages of Dr. George Pararas-Carayannis*, accessed May 25, 2022, http://www.drgeorgepc.com /Volcano1883Krakatoa.html.
2. Mary Bagley, "Krakatoa Volcano: Facts about 1883 Eruption," *Live Science*, September 14, 2017, https://www.livescience.com/28186-krakatoa.html.
3. Acts 1:8-11.
4. Acts 2:14-21.
5. Acts 2:5-7.
6. Ephesians 4:15, NASB1995.
7. 1 Corinthians 12:4-11.
8. Acts 6:3, NIV.

CHAPTER 8: RELEASE CAPTIVES

1. Exodus 13:3.
2. Colossians 1:13-14.

3. Titus 3:3-5.
4. Deuteronomy 10:17-21, NIV.
5. Luke 4:18-21, NIV.
6. 2 Corinthians 3:17-18, NIV.

CHAPTER 9: RELIEVE SOMEONE'S PAIN

1. Luke 1:46-49.
2. "'I'll Fight': 100 Years Since Booth's Final Address," *The Salvation Army National Blog*, accessed May 28, 2022, https://www.salvationarmy.org /nhqblog/news/2012-05-09-ill-fight-100-years-since-booths-final-address.
3. John 14:16, 26; 15:26; 16:7, NASB1995.
4. *Merriam-Webster*, "More Definitions for *Relief*," s.v. "relief," https://www .merriam-webster.com/dictionary/relief.
5. Acts 6:1-7.
6. James 2:8-13.
7. *Merriam-Webster*, s.v. "secure," https://www.merriam-webster.com /dictionary/secure.

CHAPTER 10: REDUCE SOMEONE'S LOAD

1. Matthew 5:38-42, NIV.
2. Mark 9:43-47.
3. Luke 22:24-27.
4. Acts 2:41-47.
5. Matthew 11:28-30.
6. Galatians 6:1-3.
7. Matthew 20:26-28.
8. Philippians 4:6-7.
9. Proverbs 27:9, NLT.
10. Proverbs 2:9-15.

CHAPTER 11: RAISE SOMEONE'S SPIRIT

1. Ephesians 6:10-18.
2. *Merriam-Webster*, s.v. "encourage," https://www.merriam-webster.com /dictionary/encourage.
3. Acts 11:23, NIV.
4. Hebrews 3:12-13, NIV.
5. Romans 14:19, NIV.
6. 2 Corinthians 12:19, NLT.
7. 2 Corinthians 10:8.

CHAPTER 12: REACH SOMEONE'S SOUL

1. "Why Some Men Struggle to Find and Maintain Friendships," *ConvoConnection*, February 12, 2020, https://www.convoconnection.com /blog/why-some-men-struggle-to-find-and-maintain-friendships. For more on male friendships, see Geoffrey Greif, *Buddy System: Understanding Male Friendships* (New York: Oxford University Press, 2008).
2. John 17:1-3.
3. To learn more about Don's story, see his book *Peace Child: An Unforgettable Story of Primitive Jungle Treachery in the 20th Century* (Ventura, CA: Regal, 2005).
4. Ecclesiastes 3:11, NIV.
5. Colossians 4:2-6.
6. Acts 4:8-12.
7. Acts 5:40.
8. Acts 5:41-42.
9. 1 Corinthians 2:1-5.
10. John 4:34-36.

APPENDIX A: THE EMPOWERING PRESENCE

1. John 7:37-38, NIV.
2. John 7:39, NIV.
3. John 14:16-17, NIV.
4. 1 Corinthians 2:12, NIV.
5. Galatians 3:3, NIV.
6. Galatians 5:17, NIV.
7. 1 Corinthians 2:14, NIV.
8. 1 Corinthians 2:15-16, NIV.
9. Romans 8:5, NLT.
10. Galatians 5:16, 25, NIV.
11. Galatians 5:22-23, NIV.
12. Ephesians 5:18, NLT.
13. 1 John 5:14-15, NIV.
14. Acts 1:8, NIV.